THE REFERENCE SHELF   VOLUME 40 NUMBER 3

THE
CONSUMING PUBLIC

EDITED BY
GRANT S. McCLELLAN

Editor, Current Magazine

THE H. W. WILSON COMPANY
NEW YORK   1968

THE REFERENCE SHELF

The books in this series contain reprints of articles, excerpts from books, and addresses on current issues and social trends in the United States and other countries. There are six separately bound numbers in each volume, all of which are generally published in the same calendar year. One number is a collection of recent speeches; each of the others is devoted to a single subject and gives background information and discussion from various points of view, concluding with a comprehensive bibliography.

Subscribers to the current volume receive the books as issued. The subscription rate is $14 in the United States and Canada ($17 foreign) for a volume of six numbers. Single numbers are $3.50 each in the United States and Canada ($4 foreign).

THE CONSUMING PUBLIC

Copyright © 1968
By the H. W. Wilson Company

Library of Congress Catalog Card No. 68-17134

PRINTED IN THE UNITED STATES OF AMERICA

PREFACE

What is the reason for the recent and growing interest in consumer problems in America? Has consumer protection been strengthened as a result of this renewed interest? And what can be expected for the future?

A seeming paradox confronts us. We have moved into what has been called a high consumption society bcause of our rising affluence. Indeed we are moving from a mass middle-class standard of living to a mass high-class standard of living. Yet at the same time the average consumer often feels frustrated, neglected, even harmed and defrauded. Though not perhaps part of the paradox, the consumer who is actually impoverished has of course much greater difficulty as he responds to his more complex consumption needs and the ever more complex market.

Against this broad setting, an attempt is made to answer the opening questions above in the first section of this compilation. In the second section the many activities of government at all levels dealing with consumer problems and consumer complaints are surveyed. The reactions of the business community are touched on in the third section. Next, a few of the outstanding consumer problems—the special problems of the poor, medical care, automobile insurance, food production—are considered. In the final section several authors take a look at new developments in the consumer interest movement and the new directions in which it appears to be moving.

The editor wishes to thank both the authors and the publishers of the following selections for permission to reprint them in this book.

GRANT S. MCCLELLAN

May 1968

CONTENTS

III.   BUSINESS AND CONSUMER PROTECTION

IV.   CONSUMER CONCERNS

V. The Consumer Interest Movement

I. THE CITIZEN AS CONSUMER

EDITOR'S INTRODUCTION

Americans have always been driven by the desire to consume more and more, first from our agricultural economy and then from the products of the industrial revolution. Now that revolution has brought us within reach of a mass high-income economy. With urbanization we have left behind early agricultural communities, even neighborhood communities and the like. We live virtually in a national "consumption community."

So argues Daniel J. Boorstin, a professor of American history at the University of Chicago, in the first selection. He notes that our drive toward ever greater consumption has always been alluded to as the materialistic streak in American culture. He counters this assumption in a novel analysis which affords a deeper understanding of much that follows in this compilation.

The remaining articles in the section deal more specifically with the nature of the mass high-income economy in which we are beginning to live and in which consumers must seek satisfaction and, necessarily, protection in its complex market arrangements.

THE CONSUMPTION COMMUNITY [1]

People tell us we are a *rich* nation. And that what distinguishes us is our *high* standard of living. But an Old World vocabulary conceals what is most radically distinctive about our material well-being. It is not that we are well off; there have been rich nations before us. It is not that we have a *high* standard of living. What is different is our very notion of a standard of living, and our New World way of thinking about and consuming material goods.

[1] From "Welcome to the Consumption Community," by Daniel J. Boorstin. *Fortune.* 76:118-20+. S. 1, '67. The author is Preston and Sterling Morton Distinguished Service Professor of American History at the University of Chicago. Copyright 1967 by Daniel J. Boorstin. Reprinted by permission. (The material in this article will be included in *The Americans: The World Experience*, the third and concluding volume of his history of American civilization, to be published by Random House.)

The movement from the Old World to the New was a movement from an ancient and traditional view of wealth to the new view that goes by the name of the standard of living. "Wealth," which was at the center of English mercantilist economic thinking before the American Revolution, was a static notion. The wealth of the world, which was measured primarily in gold and silver, was supposed to be a fixed quantity. It was a pie that could be sliced one way or another. But the size of the pie could not be substantially increased. A bigger slice for Great Britain meant a smaller slice for France or Spain or somebody else, and one nation's gain was another's loss.

The New World changed that way of thinking. People who came to live here came to better their lot in the world, to improve their "way of life." They sought opportunities to rise, to get better land, to think and speak freely, to move, to worship, to secure more education, to grow. By contrast with that of the Old World, America bred a vaguer and much more expansive view of the material world. . . .

Americans were not merely struggling for their slice of the pie, every day they were actually making the pie bigger. The indefinite expansibility of material wealth was an American axiom, never abandoned. The Old World's notions about what was material well-being, what was worth fighting about, were becoming obsolete. . . .

The ideal self-made man was the man who rose, not at the expense of others, but while building new communities where others would flourish. The slogans of "The New Freedom," "The New Deal," "The New Frontier," and "The Great Society" have carried these hopes forward into the twentieth century.

With this novel, vague, and expansive view of material well-being came a new way of talking about the wealth of the society. This new view was *communitarian*. Its focus was not on riches but on the way of life, not on the individual but on the community. Or, rather, on many novel kinds of communities. One of these, which came to dominate the twentieth century, was the byproduct of innovation in manufacturing and distributing things. To it I give the name "Consumption Community." A Consumption Community is held together by much thinner, more temporary ties than those that bound earlier Americans. It does not replace earlier kinds of communities. But it draws together in novel ways people who would not otherwise have been drawn together—people who do not share ideology, who are not voyaging together on the prairie or building new towns. It is a hallmark of American life today.

A Consumption Community consists of people who have a feeling of shared well-being, shared risks, common interests, and common concerns that come from consuming the same kinds of objects. It can be the community of Scotch drinkers who rally to the J & B brand, of three-button-suit wearers, of Chevrolet sports-car drivers, of super-king-sized cigarette smokers, or of Doublemint gum chewers. As the advertisers of nationally branded and nationally advertised products are constantly telling us, by buying their products we are joining a special group—the Dodge Rebellion, the Pepsi Generation, those who throw in their lot with Avis because it is only No. 2. And each of us eagerly joins many such groups. Yet we are slow to admit that buying these products and services actually puts us into novel—extremely attenuated, yet characteristically American—communities.

We remain imprisoned in an old-fashioned vocabulary. We still talk as if we were back in the world of the gunsmith who made his gun to suit a particular customer, in the days when nearly everybody wore home-made clothing and the few who wore store-boughten suits patronized a custom tailor. The world of the consumer and the experience of the consumer have not yet been given the dignity of "community." We readily speak of religious communities and political communities, but we have not yet learned to think of the consumer as belonging to communities or to speak of Consumption Communities.

The Man in the Store-Boughten Suit

Consumption Communities could not come into being until there were large numbers of objects being made that were, from the consumer's point of view, indistinguishable from one another. So long as a man purchased his gun from his own gunsmith, who had made the object for him alone, his use and enjoyment of his gun could not tie him to very many other people. Every gun—like other custom-made objects, such as suits or shoes—was designed partly by the buyer, and then made by the craftsman to the buyer's specifications. But when Whitney or Colt or a large manufacturing concern in Springfield began making guns, and making them in standard models by the thousands, every buyer of a Whitney or a Colt or a Springfield was risking his money (and sometimes, too, his life) with many others. American industry prospered on more and more ways of making precisely similar objects.

The needs of a large army in the Civil War produced masses of similar items, and after the war the new way of making things created the early Consumption Communities. The great development of factory-made shoes and clothing was partly a result of that war. Before the Civil War it was widely assumed that well-fitting clothes could not be manufactured in large quantities since everybody was supposed to be a different size. But makers of uniforms found that, among large numbers of men, certain sizes recurred in a regular way. . . . For the first time in modern history it became possible for thousands of men of all social classes to wear clothing of the same design, cut, and manufacture, coming from a central factory. Before the end of the nineteenth century all but a small proportion of American men were wearing store-boughten clothing.

The making of large numbers of similar objects gradually extended to all items of consumption. Cigarettes, which until the later nineteenth century had been mostly handmade, were now rolling off speedy new machines that, by the 1930's, were producing about 150 billion per year. Foods, soft drinks, and gadgets of all kinds were soon available in identical forms and in quantities that by the early twentieth century had dominated the lives of most Americans. And the supreme achievement of precise mass production was, of course, the automobile, which soon became the omnipresent symbol of American Consumption Communities. By the third decade of the century, the house that a man lived in, together with antiques and certain art works (and the land that he lived on), was almost the only object that had not become fungible—readily replaced in the market by others that were indistinguishable.

This capacity to produce millions of similar objects was necessary to the creation of Consumption Communities. But it was not enough. Community requires a *consciousness* of community. And at the same time, in the century after the Civil War, there grew in America new institutions that made men and women aware of their membership in Consumption Communities. Two large developments brought the new consciousness into being.

First came the retailing revolution. Its two principal novel agents were the department store and the mail-order house. Before the middle of the nineteenth century, city dwellers bought their goods from numerous specialized shops, each offering a relatively small stock of one kind of commodity—drygoods, hardware, groceries, crockery, or tableware. Then, in 1846, A. T. Stewart in New York City pioneered with his Marble Dry-Goods Palace at Broadway and Chambers Street. He gave a hint of the vastness and grandeur of the new retailing enterprises with his new eight-story building in 1862, which became famous as Stewart's Cast Iron Palace. Others too—R. H. Macy in New York, John Wanamaker in Philadelphia and New York, Marshall Field and Carson Pirie Scott in Chicago, and many more—combined their pioneering in large-scale retailing with pioneering in architecture. They opened new perspectives to the entering customer—long vistas of appealing merchandise, and numerous clusters of buyers, shoppers, and just lookers. These were displayed not in the motley disorder of a country fair, but as the common offering of a single great enterprise. A buyer at Stewart's or Macy's or Wanamaker's was not simply putting his confidence in the integrity of a particular shopkeeper. He was joining a large community of consumers, all of whom put their confidence (and their cash) in the same large firm. When the one-price system, popularized by R. H. Macy, took the place of the ancient custom of haggling, buyers more than ever were sharing their confidence in the merchant.

A Common Iconography in the Catalogue

What the department store was to the city dweller, the mail-order house was to the farmer. Montgomery Ward, which had begun only in 1872, issued a catalogue for 1884 that numbered 240 pages and listed over 10,000 items. Sears, Roebuck & Co., which had started as a one-man mail-order watch business in 1886, was grossing over $50 million by 1907, selling every shape and size of merchandise. In that year catalogue circulation already exceeded three million. The Ward and Sears catalogues, full of vivid illustrations (soon printed in color, in the development of which the mail-order houses were pioneers), opened the outside world to many lonely farm families. Thousands wrote in for personal advice. Buyers from the catalogue were putting their confidence in a firm located in a far-off city. It was no accident that the catalogue came to be called "the farmer's Bible." Men remote from one another found in their Sears catalogue a common iconography. They were tied together somehow by their common involvement in the large community of Sears customers.

At the same time there grew nationwide chains of poor man's department stores, 5-and-10-cent stores selling thousands of standardized small items. The customers of F. W. Woolworth shared the belief that these items could nowhere be bought more cheaply, and that they were good value for the money. This expanding confidence of the growing community of 5-and-10 customers within a few decades built what was at that time the highest building in the United States.

People who shopped at Stewart's, Macy's, Wanamaker's, or Marshall Field's, or who mailed in their orders to Ward or Sears, could see and feel that they had entered a new community of consumers. But another new force was reaching out into the city and the country, tying other groups of consumers together. It used the pages of newspapers and magazines, the painted sides of barns, signs along the road, trolley cars and buses and commuter trains, and ultimately smoke writing in the sky, and words and music and images on the airwaves of radio and television. Before the middle of the twentieth century empty spaces everywhere were being filled with words and pictures, and the channels were crammed with words and music and pictures—designed to enlist new consumers into new Consumption Communities, and to keep old consumers loyal to the Consumption Communities they had joined. This new force was, of course, advertising.

Nothing can be more misleading than to describe advertising as "salesmanship in words." True enough, advertising aims to sell. But salesmanship is aimed at the individual consumer, advertising at *groups* of consumers. Since the nineteenth century these groups have become larger and larger.

Salesmanship and Advertising Differ

There are crucial differences between selling a single buyer and creating a community of buyers. Different arguments become effective and different satisfactions are received by everyone concerned. The primary argument of the salesman is personal and private: this hat is perfect for *you* (singular). The primary argument of the advertisement is public and general: this hat is perfect for *you* (plural). The salesman is effective when he persuades the customer that the item is peculiarly suited to his unique needs. The advertisement is effective when it persuades groups of buyers that the item is well suited to the needs of all persons in the group. The salesman's focus is on the individual; he succeeds when he manages, cajoles, flatters, and overwhelms the ego. The advertisement's focus is on some group; it succeeds when it discovers, defines, and persuades persons who can be brought into that community of consumers.

A buyer who gives in to a salesman has satisfied his ego. But a consumer who is persuaded by an advertisement is also yielding to his desire or willingness to be counted in a group—a community of consumers. An advertisement is, in fact, a form of insurance to the consumer that by buying this commodity, by smoking this brand of cigarette, or driving this make of car he will not find himself alone. The larger the advertising campaign, the more widespread and the more effective, the more the campaign itself offers a kind of communitarian seal of approval. Surely a million customers can't be wrong! An advertisement, then, is a kind of announcement that, in the well-informed judgment of experts, some kind of Consumption Community probably exists. Won't you join?

Advertising—the conscious effort to create Consumption Communities—did not become an important element in the economy

and in securing customers until about a century ago. Patent medicines were the first to advertise on a national scale. But the use of
display type and illustrations in daily newspaper advertising came
in only slowly. As late as 1847, James Gordon Bennett, the otherwise enterprising editor of the New York *Herald,* banned all orna-
mental cuts. He believed in a typographic democracy—thinking it
"unfair" to allow any advertiser an advantage over others by his
use of display type. Bennett insisted that an advertiser should gain
his advantage only from what he said, not from how it was printed.
But by the later nineteenth century, newspaper and magazine pages
were responding freely to the needs of advertisers. In 1879, Wanamaker placed what is said to be the first full-page American newspaper advertisement for a retail store. In the early twentieth century
display type, illustrations, and the full-page advertisement became
commonplace.

The volume of national expenditure on advertising has increased
spectacularly and regularly, interrupted only by the deeper depres-
sions. In 1867 the total national figure was only some $50 million;
by 1900 it had increased tenfold to half a billion dollars; by 1950
it had reached five and a half billion; by 1966 it was over sixteen
billion. Since the 1930's, national advertising has increased more
rapidly than local advertising. By 1966 the annual expenditure on
local advertising was only about half that on national advertising.

Brand names first flourished about the time of the Civil War
with patent medicine, soap, and cleaning powder. By the time of
World War I, people were asking for national brands in chewing
gum, watches, hats, breakfast food, razor blades, and pianos. Advertising was becoming a technique, a science, and a profession. In
1869 appeared Rowell's *American Newspaper Directory,* the first
serious attempt to list all newspapers in the United States with
accurate and impartial estimates of their circulation. Ayer's *American Newspaper Annual* followed in 1880.

Packaging the "Uneeda Biscuit"

The advertising agency then appeared, to guide manufacturers
to the most effective use of the media. N. W. Ayer & Son of Phila-

delphia—which had started with a list of eleven religious newspapers before 1877—was a pioneer, but many others followed.
Ayer's accounts included Hires root beer, Montgomery Ward, Procter & Gamble soaps, and Burpee seeds. By 1900 the advertising of
foodstuffs held first place in the firm's volume. What was perhaps
the biggest single advertising push until then was Ayer's campaign,
beginning in January 1899, for the new National Biscuit Company.
This was one of the first campaigns to feature a staple food, nationally branded, boxed in individual packages, and ready for consumption. The campaign required the perfecting of an airtight
package, and above all the popularizing of a distinctive trademark
and brand name. Ayer reached consumers through newspapers,
magazines, streetcar ads, posters, and painted signs. Overnight
people all over the country were demanding the "Uneeda Biscuit."

Too much of the discussion of advertising has treated it as simply
another form of salesmanship. Estimates of its social value have
centered around its cost as a selling device, its relation to planned
obsolescence and to other aspects of production. We must begin
to realize that Consumption Communities actually offer many of
the satisfactions that were once associated only with other kinds
of groups.

A Bond for Americans

In its primary sense, a "community" was a group of people
living together, under all the same conditions of life. In origin it
appears to have come from the Latin *com* (together) plus the Latin
munus (service, office, function, or duty)—hence meaning persons
who paid taxes together or worked together. By extension it came
to mean persons held together by some one common interest or
concern, generally political or religious. In its primary sense, as in
the New England community, or the New York community, or the
plantation community, it meant persons who lived in geographic
proximity. But it has also come to mean any group (the business
community, the Catholic community, the Negro community, the
Jewish community, the teen-age community, the suburban community) aware of its common characteristic, and somehow held
together, even though its members do not necessarily live close to

one another. Those groups, which we commonly call "communities," show the following characteristics: (1) people are aware of their membership in the group and are aware that the membership gives them some common interests or concerns; (2) people are more or less free to enter or leave the community, if only by emigration; (3) people show more or less loyalty to some common object.

The peculiar importance of Consumption Communities in recent America helps us understand how it has been possible here to assimilate—to "Americanize"—the many millions who have come within the last century and a half. Consumption Communities helped hold together as Americans people who in the older world would have been bound mainly by distinction of class, ideology, or ancestry.

Here are some of the peculiarities of Consumption Communities—by contrast with other kinds of communities.

Consumption Community is quick. It takes generations to become an Englishman, one can never become a Frenchman. But, through joining Consumption Communities, it has been easy for immigrants to become Americans. . . .

Consumption Community is non-ideological. No profession of faith, no credo or orthodoxy, no ritual is required to join a Consumption Community. With only a few exceptions (now mostly having to do with housing), people of all races, beliefs, and religious and political creeds can join. And therefore:

Consumption Community is democratic. This is the great American democracy of cash, which so exasperates the aristocrats of all older worlds. Consumption Communities generally welcome people of all races, ancestry, occupations, and income levels, provided they have the price of admission. The boss and the worker both own a Westinghouse washer and both drive a Mustang.

The Consumption Community is even more democratic than many a "democratic" political community. English law reformers used to say, "British justice, like the Ritz Hotel, is open to Rich and Poor alike." To secure a room in the Ritz, or in other de luxe London accommodations, though, you needed not only to have enough money but also to be a "gentleman" and to be a member of the right race. The struggle for "civil rights" in the United States has been in large part a struggle for the right to consume—a struggle to enlarge and complete the democracy of consumption. The purpose of the public-accommodation provisions of the Civil Rights Acts is to ensure that the Ritz Hotel and all other hotels, motels, and restaurants are open to whoever has the money.

People who want to protest against this peculiarly indiscriminate American democracy can do so only by underconsumption. It is possible, although increasingly inconvenient, to stay out of even the largest Consumption Communities. Latter-day Boston Brahmins must strain for exclusiveness by refusing to own an automobile or a television set. I have one such acquaintance who has the hardiness not to have a telephone—on the pretext that he is waiting for it to be perfected! The democracy of cash, even with all its present limitations in America, is probably one of the most real and present and unadulterated democracies in history.

Consumption Communities tend to become the model of all other communities. All experience tends to be treated more and more like the experience of consuming. It becomes the right of all citizens not merely to consume whatever they can afford to buy, but to consume it in the presence of (and in community with) all others who can afford to buy it. And of course we use advertising to create and strengthen old-style communities—communities of believers, religious and political.

The growth of Consumption Communities has signaled a transformation of the attitude to all material goods. By contrast with the rigid, Old World notion of wealth, the New World idea of standard of living has had certain obvious characteristics. I will mention only two.

Standard of living is public. It is possible to be rich in secret. A man can hide his treasure in a vault, in his garden, in a mattress. "If rich, it is easy enough to conceal your wealth," an Englishman wrote in 1820; "it is less difficult to hide a thousand guineas than a hole in your coat." It is not possible to have a high standard of living in secret.

Well-Being Goes on Display

The word "standard" (which comes into English from the Old French *estandard*, "banner") means a symbol that is displayed for all to see. Its very function is to be seen, to inform as much as to affirm. A standard of living, then, is a publicly seen, and known measure of how people do live, and of how they should live. The first use of the phrase in its current and special American sense is obscure. But probably not until the twentieth century did the phrase come into widespread use with its present meaning.

The willingness of Americans to display their material well-being is rooted deep in our history. The fact that our homes front upon the street (and not inward to a court as did the middle-class homes of French and Spanish colonists), and that the symbols of urban residential comfort here are not the wall or the fence but the broad, open front lawn and the front porch—these are clues from small-town America of the last century. In mid-twentieth century, the Oldsmobile, Cadillac, or Continental conspicuously parked in front of the house offers new opportunities to display the well-being of the residents. But the Americans' willingness to display their prosperity on the façades of their homes, in their picture windows, on their lawns, and in the parking places in front of their houses is by no means universal. Americans who travel the Continent of Europe are sometimes shocked at the shabby exterior of the dwellings of well-to-do families of the middle class. The ancient institution of the tax farmer, who could estimate his exactions by the wealth displayed, put a premium on the ability to seem impecunious....

Freedom from the Tax Farmer

But the United States was born in the principle of "No taxation without representation." The tax farmer has not been an American institution. We have been relatively free from social revolutions and from arbitrary confiscation. Americans have therefore had less reason to fear the consequences of public display of their wealth.

Because a high standard of living is a public fact, it becomes a public benefit. You can become rich without my becoming richer. But it is hard for *you* to have a high standard of living without incidentally raising mine. The rich classes of India, protected by their eight-foot stone walls, can enjoy luxury. They do not really have a high standard of living in the American sense so long as the squalor outside their walls threatens them with crime and disease. If, in addition to your material goods, your standard of living includes your freedom from threat of crime or disease, your education, the education of your children, the air you breathe, the water you drink, the roads you drive on, the public transportation system you use, your peace of mind—then does it not inevitably include *my* opportunities and the opportunities of my children for education (in the institutions you support), the air *I* breathe, the water *I* drink, the roads *I* drive on, the public transportation *I* use, and *my* freedom from threat of crime or disease?

Standard of living is pervasive, reciprocal, and communal. This plainly follows. Wealth is by definition what a man *possesses.* Property is what is "proper" to a person, peculiar or special to him. How obvious, then, that the wealth of some should explain the poverty of others. "The pleasures of the rich," wrote the Englishman Thomas Fuller in 1732, "are bought with the tears of the poor."

But standard of living is what a man *shares.* One man's standard of living cannot be sharply separated from that of others. Each person is part of everyone else's standard of living. *You* are my environment. And my environment is my standard of living. In a society that lives by a standard of living, no man is an island, for every man is part of every other man's standard of living. In a wealth society your gain is my loss; in a standard-of-living society your gain is my gain. If you live healthily I am less likely to catch a disease. If you and others are educated and content, the crime rate declines, and that improves my standard of living. By the wealth idea, one man is poor because another man is rich; by a standard of living, one man is poor because another is poor.

It is no wonder, then, that in the mid-twentieth century, when, as never before, we are dominated by concern for our standard of living, we should give a central place to education. For the education of my neighbors, we assume, improves my human environment, and hence raises my standard of living. To build a public school may not increase my wealth; it is likely to affect my standard of living. The 1954 integration decision of the Supreme Court was based on the assumption that a standard of living is pervasive, reciprocal, and communal. It was not enough that Negroes should have access to similar instruction, or to private instruction. Equality in a standard-of-living society meant the right to be educated together with and in the presence of other Americans. The opportunities that had historically been given to white Americans could themselves benefit the Negro—but only if he received his education along with them, and in their presence.

Although standard of living is somehow a measure, and a public measure, it is necessarily vague. Wealth can be specifically and precisely defined and weighed, but standard of living has no boundaries. It includes everything in our experience—the production and distribution systems that help us acquire material goods, the climate, the air we breathe, the water we drink, our access to the woods, the richness of our thoughts, the sensitivity of our feelings, and our peace of mind.

The very notion of standard of living is cosmopolitan and universalizing. Just as the Old World mercantilist idea of wealth (essentially treasure) drove toward autarky and competition among nations, so the American idea of standard of living drives us toward cooperation and world community. In the long run, our ability to raise our American standard of living will depend on our ability to remove the menaces to our health and peace of body and mind, which come from the dissatisfactions and lack of satisfactions of men anywhere.

The Sharing Experience

In the eighteenth century, nations believing the mercantilist dogma organized their laws and commerce to prevent other nations from acquiring their know-how. Jefferson had to smuggle rice seeds out of France and Italy. The plans for the first weaving machines had to be illegally exported from England; it was unlawful for a skilled workman to leave the country. By contrast, in the twentieth century the Marshall plan, Point IV, and other aid programs express our belief that peace and prosperity may depend on our ability to raise the standard of living of others. What could more dramatically express our belief in the communal character of material well-being?

It is misleading, then, to think of "conspicuous consumption" as a pathological expression of the oddities of the rich or the perverse. In the United States in the mid-twentieth century nearly all consumption has become conspicuous. Private consumption is the phenomenon of wealth societies. Ours is a standard-of-living society. How otherwise than by public consumption can one signal his membership in Consumption Communities? We learn how to consume, how to join these communities, by seeing how others consume. Advertisers seek to inform us of Consumption Communities and to persuade us to join them. Each of us informs other consumers of our loyalty to these Consumption Communities simply by showing how we consume. The sharing experience that comes to groups of us because we consume the same brands, comes to all of us because we share a standard of living.

To speak of American "materialism" is, then, both an understatement and a misstatement. The material goods that historically have been the symbols which elsewhere separated men from one another have become, under American conditions, symbols which hold men together. From the moment of our rising in the morning, the breakfast food we eat, the coffee we drink, the automobile we drive to work—all these and nearly everything we consume becomes a thin, but not negligible, bond with thousands of other Americans.

When the impoverished cannot afford to consume like others they are not merely deprived—they are excluded. They become outsiders because they are not linked by bonds that unite other Americans.

Consumption Communities, both by their strengths and by their weaknesses, reveal to us peculiar features of American life in our time. Older forms of community—of family, of nation, and of religion—of course still continue to bind men together. But the distinctive twentieth-century form of community evolved in modern America is the Consumption Community—measured and displayed in a standard of living.

THE MASS HIGH-INCOME CONSUMERS [2]

The United States was the first nation in which economic growth transformed the mass consumer market from a low-income to a middle-income market. This phase of economic evolution is now ending, and the United States is entering the era of the mass *high*-income market. By 1975, on *Fortune*'s projections, average family income after Federal taxes will be around $10,000. Even today, 21 million families have incomes over $10,000, and they account for well over half of total income in the United States. This spread of affluence is transforming consumer markets, and clearly has enormous implications for markets of the future.

Incomes cannot be expected to rise quite as rapidly in the eight years between now and 1975 as they did during the past eight years. In this recent period, real disposable income rose about 43 per cent. (Just since 1963, with the economy pushed along by a cyclical upturn and the effects of the Vietnam war, the advance came to 25 per cent.) For the next eight years it is reasonable to expect that total real income will increase by more than a third. And with so many families now beyond the point where spending must go entirely for necessities, and able to exercise some discretion about what they buy, the stream of "discretionary income" will swell by considerably more than a third.

It is of course no secret that affluence is spreading in the United States. But data on the distribution of personal income after Federal taxes—how many family units receive how much of this income—have not been available since the Department of Commerce stopped publishing such data several years ago; its last figures are for 1962. *("Family units" include families in the ordinary sense of the word, plus individuals living alone or with other, unrelated, persons. [People in institutions and some members of the armed forces are excluded.] It is roughly accurate to refer to all units with incomes of $10,000 or more as "families," since relatively few individuals not living with their own families have that much income.) Fortune* undertook a considerable statistical effort to estimate the U.S.

[2] From "The Diverse $10,000-and-Over Masses," by Lawrence A. Mayer, an associate editor of *Fortune. Fortune.* 76:114-17+. D. '67. Reprinted from the December 1967 issue of *Fortune* Magazine by special permission; © 1967 Time Inc.

income distribution as of 1967 and, building on this and other information, to project the figures ahead to 1975. As was the case in the Commerce estimates, capital gains were not taken into account. It was assumed in making the projections that there would be no severe recession or large-scale war, and that national productivity would continue to gain at an average rate of about 3 per cent a year. To eliminate the distorting effects of inflation, all of the income data were converted into constant dollars, based on 1967 purchasing power; the estimates and projections in this article are stated in these 1967 dollars.

One finding of the *Fortune* analysis is that the lower income brackets are shrinking noticeably, in general confirming the widespread impression that the number of persons living in "poverty" has been falling. The number of family units with incomes below $5,000 declined by something like four million from 1959 to 1967. Over the same span the number with incomes between $5,000 and $7,500 also declined, by about three million. The total of the two categories, 38 million family units in 1959, is down to 31 million [1967]. The number of under-$7,500 units will continue to decline in the next eight years, although at a somewhat slower rate. One reason for the slowdown is that the number of people in their middle, most productive years will show no growth at all, while the ranks of both young adults and of older people, who typically receive lower than average incomes, will be swelling. Another reason is that a residue of families headed by persons who are sick, uneducated, or discriminated against, or otherwise handicapped, will find it difficult to climb to $7,500 even by 1975.

A Large Market in a Once-Thin Layer

Moving up the income scale, the $7,500-to-$10,000 group, eight million family units in 1959, has grown to 9.7 million and will grow about as much in the next eight years. Somewhat more family units are pushing their way up and into this class than are pushing up and out into a higher bracket. Within the bracket, life styles vary considerably. While an urban family of five living on $7,500 is apt to feel somewhat pinched, single individuals in this bracket are rather well-off—and there are about a million of them.

The big news about U.S. incomes these days is the extraordinary rise of those $10,000-and-over units. Their numbers are increasing much faster than the total number of family units. Eight years ago 17 per cent of all family units had incomes of $10,000 or more after Federal taxes. Today the figure is up to about 35 per cent. In 1975 it will be approaching 50 per cent—as these figures (rounded to the nearest million) make clear:

	Family Units (in millions)		
	1959	1967	1975
Total	55	62	72
$10,000 and over	10	21	34

The bulk of the growth is occurring in the $10,000-to-$15,000 subgroup. Only 5 million families were in that bracket in 1959, but the number is already up to 14 million and will be around 22 million in 1975. By that year there will actually be about as many families with $10,000 to $15,000 as with $5,000 to $10,000. Even the once-thin layer above, the families with more than $15,000, is coming to constitute quite a large market. The number of families above $15,000 has grown from 4.5 million in 1959 to 7.5 million today; by 1975 it will swell to 12 million. Of these families, about two million will have from $20,000 to $25,000, and perhaps 1.5 million will have more than $25,000.

In some ways the new consumer market is even richer than the foregoing statistics indicate. The $10,000-and-over families carry more weight than their numbers suggest. Their *average* income this year is a hefty $15,000, three times the average for all other family units. When looked at in terms of the total dollars they command, *the $10,000-and-over families already dominate the American market.* In 1959 they accounted for 40 per cent of all income. This year they account for a bit over 60 per cent. By 1975 their share should top 70 per cent.

These rising percentages translate into enormous gains in buying power. In 1959 the $10,000-and-over classes had a total income of $150 billion or so. This year it comes to about $330 billion. In 1975 it will come to roughly $520 billion. The case may be viewed this way: in 1975, families with at least $10,000 will have more income—$145 billion more, in fact—than *all* families had in 1959.

The Rise of the White Coveralls

The massive growth of the $10,000-or-more income group has in part resulted from shifts in the occupational structure of the labor force, i.e., from shifts into more skilled, higher-paying jobs (as opposed to the growth based on higher pay for the same jobs). However, effects of the occupational shifts have not been as great as one might suppose, given all the attention paid in recent years to the shift from blue-collar to white-collar jobs.

Those whom the United States Government classifies as "professional, technical, and kindred workers" and as "managers, officials, and proprietors" together constitute little more than one fifth of all employed persons, but people in such occupations head about two fifths of all of the families with incomes of $10,000 or more. These proportions have stayed essentially unchanged during recent years even though the professional, technical, and kindred group, the most highly paid of all, has grown at a faster rate than all others. The explanation is that the broad government categories contain many different kinds of jobs. It turns out, in fact, that of the nearly ten million workers in the professional, technical, and kindred group, no more than half have incomes of $10,000 or more. While the ranks of such professionals as biologists, mathematicians, physicists, psychologists, and certain kinds of engineers are growing especially fast, the absolute numbers in these occupations remain small. Meanwhile, some very large "semiprofessional" groups, such as technicians who assist scientists, engineers, and the like, medical and dental technicians, and a whole variety of miscellaneous categories, are growing very rapidly too, and a good many of the people employed in these occupations earn less than $10,000 (many are women, many are young people). But increasing numbers of the semiprofessional jobs in offices, laboratories, colleges, medical institutions, research installations, and the like are going to be paying $10,000 or more in the years ahead as the demand for skilled backup personnel continues to mount.

The semiprofessionals are beginning to make themselves felt as a distinct force in consumer markets. Many of the younger ones are educated enough, affluent enough, and confident enough of their futures to be among the consumption leaders of the day—those who eagerly adopt the latest fashions, buy sporty cars, take ski vacations in Europe. As time goes on, more and more marketing men will have to draw a bead on these semiprofessionals, or "white coveralls," as they have been called. . . .

The Option of Not Buying

The affluent families, then, have become a quite diverse group that includes a whole spectrum of occupations and encompasses rather wide differences in education and social class. What these families chiefly have in common is enough income to be able to exercise broad options in disposing of their income; and because they have so much of the total income in the United States, the options they exercise have great impact on the whole consumer market. . . .

There is difficulty in projecting future savings patterns from data on the relation between savings and income in some past year, so it is difficult to project expenditures from such data. Nevertheless, it is instructive to look at some BLS [Bureau of Labor Statistics] figures for 1960-61 as a point of departure. In capsule, here is what they show. High-income families at that time devoted a perceptibly larger proportion of their expenditures than lower-income families to alcoholic beverages, recreation, and education. Their outlays on clothing, eating out, and travel were particularly higher than average. The spending share for food eaten at home was less than in other groups; that for buying of automobiles declined above the $15,000 mark. The high-income groups as a whole spent a relatively smaller than average share on housing, including utilities and all other matters connected with the house. But in the topmost group ($15,000 and over) the proportion spent for housing went up. This was mainly because the BLS housing figures include outlays for household help, outside laundering and cleaning, repairs, and in the high-income groups these outlays run relatively high.

The Scotch and Silver Buyers

With all the qualifications that have to be made in using such data for forecasting, it is still hard to imagine that certain particular markets won't benefit from plentiful income. Prime specific examples are Scotch, sterling silver, furs, pianos and organs, tickets to concerts and plays, private-school tuition, car rentals, and boating.

Efforts to project the effects of rising levels of affluence on patterns of consumer outlays are further complicated by differences between families with the same income. A notable kind of difference is that between white-collar and blue-collar families. The BLS data show that in 1960-61 blue-collars spent differently from professionals and managers of the same income level. Blue-collar families laid out more for tobacco and automobiles than the upper-status families, and less for cultural activities and housing. Lower expenditures on housing—including home furnishings—have been explained by Social Research Inc., headed by Dr. Burleigh B. Gardner, as resulting from the propensity of working-class wives to seek mostly "comfort" while middle-class wives are more interested in appearance, "something that conveys a visual impression that corresponds to some more or less explicit standard of taste."

Patterns of consumer behavior associated with social status are slow to change, and their extent and durability can easily be underestimated. Some years back, for example, it was widely believed that in moving beyond the city line many millions of people were adopting the same set of suburban manners, morals, and spending habits. Later research suggests that this just isn't so, that suburbia does not "homogenize" its inhabitants. There are diverse suburbs, and if a particular suburb seems homogeneous, that is probably because it is inhabited by people who were socially and economically alike to begin with.

Beyond Yesterday's Boundaries

Nevertheless, there is *some* tendency toward convergence in consumer habits, in cities and suburbs too. For example, blue-collar people eat out more often than they used to, and they increasingly buy the same kinds of apparel as white-collar people. And for all kinds of families, a move to suburbia does involve certain appurtenances—at least one car, outdoor play equipment for children, the paraphernalia of lawn care.

While there is some tendency for class differences in consumer behavior to wane, powerful forces are making for greater diversity in consumer choices. Every day, it seems, American consumers have a greater variety to select from. New products and designs as well as novelties and fads come along in swift procession. This plentitude itself encourages people to express their individuality as consumers, move beyond yesterday's boundaries, and buy things they haven't bought before. . . .

A Leisure-Oriented Pattern

Another kind of choice that affluence can make possible is between more income and more leisure. One of the beckoning rewards of money has traditionally been leisure in which to enjoy it. For the working class, there has been a long-term trend toward shorter work weeks and, more recently, a trend toward more paid leisure too— longer vacations, even sabbaticals (e.g., for steelworkers with high seniority).

In their recent book, *The Year 2000,* Herman Kahn and Anthony J. Wiener of the Hudson Institute contemplate the possibility of a "leisure-oriented" work pattern, with a seven-and-a-half-hour day, a four-day week, thirteen weeks a year off, and ten legal holidays. The total number of work hours a year for a full-time worker would come to 1,100, not quite 60 per cent as many as now.

On a straight-line trend, the Kahn-Wiener scenario implies that by 1975 the work year would be reduced by something like 200 hours—roughly four hours a week, equivalent to more than a month of additional vacation. It seems unlikely that a decline that large will come about over so short a span of years. Agriculture aside, the work week hasn't been reduced that much in the past generation. The really significant reductions have occurred as a result of major social decisions: the cut from twelve hours a day to ten in the nineteenth century, the advent of the eight-hour day and the five-day week in the first third of this century.

But even if overwhelming amounts of leisure are not likely for a while yet, the average work year will doubtless shrink somewhat. For example, as additional income becomes more marginal, workers will seek less overtime and moonlighting income. Movement in that direction is already visible in statistics on moonlighting: the number of people holding down two or more jobs, about 3.6 million is no greater now than the number was ten years ago.

Whether or not people trade off much income for leisure, it is virtually certain that a larger and larger share of total consumer income will go for leisure or leisure-related expenditures—sporting goods, camping equipment, travel, and admissions to games, shows, and cultural events. A great many families, it can be expected, will be acquiring second homes for weekend or vacation use.

Along with greater income, and a greater variety of consumer choice, the coming of the $10,000 average-family income will be accompanied by some heightening tensions. The widening disparity between the incomes of the prosperous masses and the poor will bring increased pressures for measures to shift a larger share of total income toward the bottom of the scale. (The share of income received by the lowest fifth of all family units has not improved since the days of the New Deal.) As things are going, the feeling of deprivation is bound to mount. The average annual income of family units with $5,000 or less after taxes is now about 31 per cent of the average income of all family units; this ratio will decline to approximately 27 per cent in 1975. Since capital gains are not taken account of in these statistics, these percentages somewhat understate the actual disparities.

The Imbalance in Services

The prosperous masses will also be encountering a different sort of tension, for which it is hard to imagine any effective remedy. As more and more people become affluent, demand for some things comes greatly to exceed supply, and these are often things whose supply cannot easily be expanded. The effect of so many dollars chasing a limited supply is evident in the dizzying inflation of prices for certain kinds of nonreproducible goods such as works of art and antiques. More widespread in its effect is the growing imbalance between the supply of and the demand for certain services. The list of services already in short supply includes household help, resort reservations during the peak season, space in marinas, and tickets to various attractions, including plays, professional football games, the Metropolitan Opera. . . .

[The broad question is] whether aggregate demand will be sufficient over the next several years to sustain full-employment growth of the economy. Though blurred at present by the special effects of Vietnam-war requirements on the economy, this remains a pertinent question for the future. The adequacy of demand will to some extent depend on how desirable consumers find the goods and services available to them to purchase. At any rate, businessmen involved in supplying consumer goods and services can look forward to a very big stream of income to fish in.

TODAY'S LIVING STANDARDS [3]

The Government provided a new measure of the nation's living standards . . . [in October 1967] in a report showing a sharp rise in the amount of money city families need to achieve a moderate way of life.

The Bureau of Labor Statistics . . . said that the amount of money a typical city worker's family needed to live moderately had risen by 50 per cent since 1959 to more than $9,000 a year.

The agency said that most of the increase came because consumers were upgrading their spending habits to accompany rising earnings. A smaller amount of the increase reflected rising prices.

Arthur M. Ross, Commissioner of Labor Statistics, said that spending appeared to have risen in tandem with earnings and that for the average consumer the economic squeeze today was about the same as it was in 1959. "This means that the expectations [of consumers] have kept up with the growth of productive power," Mr. Ross said. . . . "Psychologically, they're under as much pressure as ever."

[3] From "A Family's Needs Found 50% Higher," by David R. Jones, Washington reporter. New York *Times*. p 1+. O. 25, '67. © 1967 by The New York Times Company. Reprinted by permission.

The Government report said that the biggest budget for moderate living in any mainland area was needed in the New York-northeastern New Jersey region, where the figure was $10,195.

New York jumped to first place from thirteenth place in 1959, the report said, largely because of the introduction of costs for owning a home rather than renting, plus the expansion of the geographic area outside New York City.

The budget level needed for moderate living was generally higher in the northeastern states than in most other areas, although some western cities also reported high levels. The highest for the United States was Alaska, whose specific figure was not reported, and the next highest was Honolulu, where the figure was $11,190.

Shifting Demand of Buyers

The report painted a picture of shifting consumer demands, including the strong trend since 1959 toward home and automobile ownership. It also took into account a shift to more casual clothing, dining out, dental care, smoking and alcohol and wine drinking.

Mr. Ross emphasized that the report was based on the financial needs of a so-called standard four-member family, and that the needs of other families would differ considerably depending upon their makeup. But he said the standard used in the report was a logical benchmark from which to compute the needs of other families.

The report said the standard budget "reflects the collective judgment of families as to what is necessary and desirable to meet the conventional and social as well as the physical needs of families of the budget type in the present decade."

The report, the first of its kind since 1959, is aimed at providing a useful measure of the trends of living standards. It could be used in collective bargaining, in setting criteria for such diverse things as public assistance and college scholarships, and in demands for a redefinition of the poverty level in the nation.

The standard family used as a foundation for the report was a four-member family with an employed husband thirty-eight years old, an unemployed wife, a thirteen-year-old daughter, and a thirteen-year-old son. The same standard was used in studies in 1959 and 1951.

The report said that the annual cost for this family to maintain a "moderate" living standard averaged $9,191 in urban areas last fall. The average was $9,376 in metropolitan areas and $8,366 in smaller cities, the report said.

Goods and services needed for living totaled $7,329 a year for the standard family, the report said. That excluded personal income and Social Security taxes, occupational expenses, gifts, contributions and basic life insurance.

Couple Without Children

A young couple without children would need only $3,591 to meet the same basic expenses, the report said. The cost would be at least $8,282 if the two children were of high school age, it said, and a family with four children under sixteen would need $9,674 to maintain the standard, it said.

The report estimated that the standard family needing an income of $9,191 for a moderate living last year had actually earned at least $11,000.

This meant that the family earned 16 per cent to 20 per cent more than the budget demanded, it said, which was about in line with the 15 per cent to 20 per cent surplus reported in the 1959 study.

"Thus, the standard of the new budget is at approximately the same relative position on the current scale of consumption as were the standards of the original and interim budgets" of 1951 and 1959, the study said. This prompted Mr. Ross to make his comments about the tandem rise in earnings and spending.

Dollar Figures for 1959

The report said that 23.2 cents of the typical family's dollar is spent on food, 24.1 cents on housing, 8.9 cents for transportation, 10.6 cents for clothing and personal care, 5.1 cents for medical care, 7.8 cents for other family consumption, 2.8 cents for gifts and contributions, 1.7 cents for life insurance, 0.9 cents for occupational expenses, 3.1 cents on Social Security and disability payments, and 11.8 cents on personal taxes.

In 1959, the family spent 27 cents of the dollar for food, 24 cents for housing, 8 cents for transportation, 11 cents on clothing and personal care, 5 cents on medical care, and 9 cents on other family consumption; . . . 15.7 cents went for gifts, contributions, life insurance, occupational expenses, personal taxes, and Social Security and disability payments.

II. THE ROLE OF GOVERNMENT AS PROTECTOR

EDITOR'S INTRODUCTION

Our governmental units—Federal, state and local—have always protected consumer interests in a variety of ways. We have long had postal inspection arrangements, licensing in the marketplace, antitrust legislation, the setting of product standards. Within the past three years, however, government action on behalf of consumers has greatly expanded.

Local and state government agencies have been involved and consumer counsel units have been established in them. The most dramatic action, however, has been taken by the Federal Government with the creation of a President's Committee on Consumer Interests and the appointment of a Special Assistant for Consumer Affairs at the White House level, and the appointment of a Federal Consumer Counsel to work directly under the United States Attorney General. New national legislation has been passed on such matters as safety standards in automobile design, "truth-in-packaging," "truth-in-lending," and meat inspection. In addition, tighter controls over the production and advertising of drugs and food have been enacted.

The section opens with a speech by Senator Gaylord Nelson (Democrat, Wisconsin) in which he sketches the broad obligations to consumers he believes the Government must fulfill in today's complex economy. Next, a rundown on the many Federal Government agencies involved in consumer protection is given by the editors of the *Congressional Digest*. The six following articles discuss some of the problems dealt with by recent congressional legislation. In two reports, those on truth-in-packaging and truth-in-lending, the new laws are criticized for not being more comprehensive and effective. On May 22, 1968, a more comprehensive truth-in-lending bill was approved by Congress. Its supporters agree that it is one of the strongest consumer protection measures in recent history.

Next the role of two Government agencies are explained in three articles by newspaper reporters: Nan Robertson and John D. Morris, of the New York *Times,* writing on the President's Special Assistant for Consumer Affairs and on her objectives, and John D. Morris reporting on the President's current proposals for further legislation.

The comments of the Attorney General of the State of New York, Louis J. Lefkowitz, illustrate the measures for consumer protection that can be taken at the state level.

The section closes with two critiques of government action in consumer protection to date. The first, by Max E. Brunk, Professor of Marketing, Cornell University, takes a negative view of much further governmental regulatory action. The second, by Ralph Nader, who has become a virtual one-man crusade for consumer protection, argues the case for far more government action.

THE GOVERNMENT AS REFEREE [1]

Never before in the history of our nation has there been such a critical need for the government to protect the rights of the people in their role as consumers.

The American consumer is in grave danger of becoming a casualty of bigness. The production of vital goods and services is becoming more and more the work of large, conglomerate corporations. Mass media advertising is developing consumer tastes and preferences. Modern merchandising techniques emphasize high sales volumes, rapid inventory turnover, and what is often irreverently referred to as planned obsolescence.

In this multibillion-dollar world of high speed, high pressure manufacturing, advertising, and selling, what chance does the individual consumer have to express his real preference and to get what he wants at a reasonable price? . . .

Our democratic system of government must lend a helping hand to our consumers in the modern marketplace. Elected representatives of the people must write rules of fair play, and then the government must serve as a referee to make certain that these rules are fairly observed by all.

[1] From remarks to Consumer Assembly, November 2, 1967, Washington, D.C., by Senator Gaylord Nelson (Democrat, Wisconsin). Text supplied by Senator Nelson. Senate Office Bldg. Washington, D.C. 20510. '67.

One of the responsibilities of government is to decide where and when it is necessary to play this role of referee. Let me give some outstanding examples.

First, I think we have an obligation to protect the consumer against *outright fraud*. I know of no theory of free enterprise which guarantees a furnace salesman the right to sell a widow an unneeded new heating plant on the false claim that he is a "city inspector" and that her furnace is about to explode. I know of no possible defense for door-to-door hucksters who promise a homeowner a fancy siding job free if he will simply recommend some other customers, and who then slap a second mortgage on the home and peddle it to a financial institution at a big discount. I think only vigorous prosecution and stiff penalties will put a stop to the fraud and deception which soils the marketplace today. And I don't think any reputable businessman will complain if frauds and cheats are put out of business for good.

Secondly, I think we have an obligation to guarantee the consumer a *fair choice*. I think we must accord him the dignity of knowing what he wants, and we must help him to get it. That is why we need truth-in-packaging and truth-in-lending legislation—to help assure the consumer the right to a free choice. When we bought a pound of prunes from a barrel in a general store, it was fairly easy to know what we were getting. But how does the housewife know that the Super Economy $39\frac{1}{2}$-ounce package at 3 for $1.87 is a poorer buy than the less ballyhooed, $21\frac{1}{4}$-ounce package sitting alongside it? How does the proud father, buying a television set for his kids, know that the $10 a week "easy credit" plan he is offered by the Giveaway Discount Store will triple the price of the appliance? We must insist that the manufacturer, the retailer, and the money lender give the people the facts so that they can select the product they really want, and pay a price they can understand.

Next, we have an obligation to insist on *minimum quality standards* in those products which directly affect public health and safety. We have long recognized that no one has an inherent right to sell diseased meat or contaminated milk. It certainly follows that no one has an inherent right to sell an automobile with built-in safety defects, or a tire which would be expected to fail in normal daily use. There clearly is no right to sell unsafe drugs, or poisons too dangerous to be used by the general public. We must protect not only the potential buyers from unsafe products but also the thousands of innocent citizens whom those buyers could harm once a dangerous product was in their hands. I am proud to report that the new traffic safety law which we passed just a year ago has already led to the recall of more than four million automobiles for suspected safety defects—and that these recalls have been publicly announced as required by the law.

Next, I think we have an obligation to extend the helping hand to those who need *special assistance* in today's complicated marketplace. The poor, the very young and the very old, the uneducated, the newcomer to our shores cannot be expected to compete on equal terms with a typical sophisticated American. We need consumer counsels to advise them and to help them through the bewilderment of modern society. We need legal aid programs which can guide them through our jammed and complex court procedures, whether they can afford it or not. We need to remember that our Constitution proposes "justice," and not "every man for himself."

Finally, in listing the areas where government must write the rules of fair play, I don't think we can forget government itself. The consumer's right to a fair break in the supermarket, or in the automobile agency, or in the bank or the drug store, is no greater than his right to a fair break at the city hall, the state capitol and in Washington, D.C. If we demand fair and equal treatment in the marketplace, why do we not provide fair and equal treatment in the tax office?

Consider some of the flaws in the consumer's dealings with his Federal Government. In the last report available from the Library of Congress, we are told that 19 individuals with incomes of more than $1 million a year apiece, paid no Federal tax whatsoever. Another 463 citizens with incomes of more than $1 million a year paid less than 30 per cent of their income in taxes. By comparison, those who earn $10,000 to $15,000 a year pay more than 20 per cent of their income in taxes. How can we justify taxing a $10,000 a year family more than 20 per cent of its badly needed income, and taxing a millionaire less than 30 per cent?

Of all these areas in which I have said the people's elected representatives must insist on rules of fair play, none seems more vital today than the buying and selling of prescription drugs. For six months now, our Senate Monopoly Subcommittee has been holding hearings into the buying and selling of drugs. We don't claim to be medical experts. We fully accept the greatness of the American medical profession and the pharmaceutical industry which has brought lifesaving drugs to millions of citizens to prolong their lives and ease their pain. We are merely looking at the price structure, and the facts are shocking. It seems clear that the pricing structure in the drug industry needs to be revised. There simply is not enough genuine competition in the American market. Where there is competition, prices are brought down to a tiny fraction of the price charged to the neighborhood pharmacist.

Here are some of the facts which we have uncovered:

One of the largest pharmaceutical firms, CIBA, sells the popular hypertension drug, reserpine, to the pharmacist at $39.50 per 1,000 tablets. This firm wanted to get into the New York market, so it offered this same drug to New York City hospitals at $1.10. The price to the pharmacist was 3,500 per cent higher than the price to New York City under competitive bidding. But even by cutting its price from $39.50 to $1.10, CIBA was not successful on the New York City bid. It lost out to a firm which bid 72 cents. So competition brought the price of that drug down from $39.50 to 72 cents, at least for New York City's purchases.

For another example, take prednisone, an arthritis drug. The Schering Company sells this drug to our pharmacists at $170 per 1,000. The company wanted to sell to New York City so it bid $12— but it lost the competitive bidding to a firm which bid $4.58. Then Schering turns around and sells this drug to pharmacists in Switzerland for $43.70—the same drug for which it charges our pharmacists $170.

Prednisone is a good example to cite. The authoritative publication called the *Medical Letter* reports that it tested prednisone from twenty-two different firms. The *Medical Letter* reports that "all of them conform fully to the requirements of the U.S. Pharmacopoeia," and that "there is nothing either in reports of clinical trials or in the experience of *Medical Letter* consultants to suggest that variations in formulation are causing any problems in the treatment of patients." [The U.S. Pharmacopoeia is an official compendium of drug information, giving standards of purity and strength for each compound included. *Pharmacopoeia of the United States of America.* 17th rev. ed. Mack Pub. Co. Easton, Pa. 18042. '65.—Ed.]

With that kind of expert medical assurance of the equality of these various brands of prednisone, take a look at the price structure —the price charged to the pharmacist. It ranges all the way from $5.90 to $170. The *Medical Letter* makes the obvious conclusion. It states that "the great price spread suggests the desirability of prescribing by generic name and specifying—at least for patients of limited means—that the prescription be filled with low-priced prednisone tablets.

These are the facts which our committee is developing in an effort to introduce wholesome, free enterprise competition into all aspects of drug purchasing.

We are told that, where life-saving drugs are concerned, "price is no object." Isn't it? Where is price more significant than when an ailing, elderly couple is struggling to provide itself with pain-killing, life-prolonging drugs on a meager income? Where is price more significant than in our overcrowded, underfinanced public hospitals, which are fighting to serve some of the people forgotten by the rest of society and operating on a painfully meager budget? We must make certain that the miracles of modern medicine are available to them at fair and reasonable prices. And that is the goal to which our committee is dedicated. Let me assure you, we will not be turned aside.

THE SCOPE OF FEDERAL ACTIVITY [2]

Many agencies of the Federal Government perform functions or provide services which, within a broad definition of the term *consumer*, are oriented toward the consuming public. Listed below are a number of such agencies, together with descriptions of their

[2] "The Scope of Present Federal Activity." *Congressional Digest.* 47:68-70. Mr. '68. Reprinted by permission.

consumer-related activities. Where appropriate, applicable Cabinet-level departments of the Federal Government are given in parentheses.

Administration on Aging (HEW [Health, Education and Welfare]): Strengthens and assists state and local agencies concerned with the problems of aging, including consumer problems.

Agricultural Research Service (USDA [United States Department of Agriculture]): Protects food and fiber supplies from disease and pests. Regulates marketing of pesticides. Breeds better crops, livestock, and ornamentals. Finds new consumer uses for agricultural products. Devises balanced diets; disseminates nutrition information, including calorie and vitamin content of food.

Bureau of Family Services (HEW): Provides for financial assistance, through state agencies, for needy families with dependent children. Provides for financial support, through state agencies, for needy individuals and families not covered by Medicare and other services. Provides for advice and counseling on a wide variety of personal and family matters as home management, child care, marital discord, homemaking and budgeting.

Bureau of Federal Credit Unions (HEW): Grants Federal credit union charters to qualified groups. Regulates the operations of federally chartered credit unions throughout the country to ensure sound operation for members.

Bureau of Labor Statistics (Labor): Provides technical information on cost of living, family expenditures and standards of living.

Bureau of Public Roads (Commerce): Improves highway systems in cooperation with the states. Surveys and constructs roads on public lands, such as parks, forests and defense installations. Stimulates improvement of auxiliary facilities such as freeway lighting, snow and ice removal and electronic guidance systems. Develops and promotes programs for highway safety.

Children's Bureau (HEW): Helps states extend and improve their maternal and child health, crippled children's, and child welfare services. Provides comprehensive health care for preschool and school children, particularly in areas with concentrations of low-income families. Provides medical care to women who during the maternity period are unlikely to receive necessary health care because of low incomes or for other reasons. Health care for mothers and infants following childbirth is included. Issues guides and publications for parents, teenagers, and professional personnel. Conducts research in child health and welfare problems.

Civil Aeronautics Board: Encourages development of an air transportation system that fits the needs of commerce, national defense, postal service, and the general public. Promotes efficient service at reasonable charge. Provides for enough competition to assure sound growth of air service to meet the public need. Assists in development of international air service.

Consumer and Marketing Service (USDA): Assures that meat, poultry and their products in interstate commerce are wholesome, fully and truthfully labeled, and free of disease. Provides a system of grading food products to indicate quality, size, shape, etc. Safeguards competition and fairness in the marketing of farm products. Provides money to help buy milk and other foods for school children for breakfasts and lunches and donates food for needy adults and school children. Supplies food stamps to increase food buying power of low-income families. Alerts consumers to foods currently abundant and likely to be good buys.

Department of Defense: Among its other functions, DOD protects military personnel as consumers of commercial products and services, by prescribing certain minimum standards, thereby affecting some consumer services to the public because of the large number of business firms involved. Provides free burial to military veterans and their immediate family. Sets standards for procurement of supplies that may affect standards of quality available to the public because of the large quantities purchased. Arranges for civil defense. Provides a wide variety of civil functions for the public benefit through the United States Army Corps of Engineers.

Environmental Science Services Administration (Commerce): Forecasts the weather and warns of floods, hurricanes, tornadoes and blizzards. Provides nautical and aeronautical charts, many of which are useful in recreational pursuits.

Federal Aviation Agency (Transportation): Promotes air transport safety and insures efficient operation of air transportation. Promotes development of supersonic transport. Establishes safety standards for air operations. Conducts research into all phases of aviation safety.

Federal Communications Commission: Assures that adequate facilities are available at reasonable rates to meet the needs of the public and for interstate and foreign communication service. Regulates the number and type of radio and TV stations and community antenna television (CATV) services. Sees that holders of licenses operate in the public interest. This includes seeing that stations are reasonably responsive to needs of their areas, that they do not present one side only of public controversial issues to the exclusion of others, and that they observe reasonable standards as to length, number, and loudness of commercials and that they avoid false or misleading advertising.

Federal Deposit Insurance Corporation: Insures deposits in banks of deposit which are eligible for Federal deposit insurance. The insurance covers deposits of every kind (whether public or private), including regular commercial deposits, time deposits, savings deposits, and trust funds awaiting investment. The maximum protection to a depositor in an insured bank is $15,000.

Federal Extension Service (USDA): Extends practical consumer information mostly evolving out of research done by Government, land-grant universities and private industry to families and individuals.

Federal Home Loan Bank Board: Insures holders of accounts in member savings and loan institutions up to a maximum of $15,000. Prevents unsound practices by federally chartered and state chartered savings and loan institutions insured by the FSLIC [Federal Savings and Loan Insurance Corporation].

Federal Housing Administration (HUD [Housing and Urban Development]): Brings home ownership within reach of people who otherwise might not be able to afford it, through insurance on loans. Provides means of repairing and improving houses on borrowed funds. Assures house purchasers of quality construction. Stabilizes interest rates and improves availability of mortgage money in the housing market. Provides rent supplements to needy persons.

Federal Power Commission: Regulates rates charged at the wholesale level by electricity and gas producers in interstate commerce. Regulates construction of interstate pipelines and hydro-electric projects. Insures adequate supplies for the present and anticipated needs of the public. Stimulates development of water resources for production of electric power. Stimulates development of public recreational facilities at hydroelectric projects. Promotes interconnection and coordination of electric systems to assure adequate supplies with the greatest possible economy and utilization and conservation of natural resources.

Federal Trade Commission: Prevents false and deceptive advertising. Prevents price-fixing and other business practices that are unfair to business or consumers. Assures truthful labels on wool, fur and textile products (and since the July 1, 1967, effective date of the Fair Labeling and Packaging Law of 1966, on most other commodities except foods, drugs, pesticides, seeds, and alcoholic beverages). Prevents sale of dangerously flammable wearing apparel.

Food and Drug Administration (HEW): Ensures the safety and effectiveness of drugs and therapeutic devices by requiring substantial proof of these qualities from the manufacturer; ensures that the procedures used for manufacturing drugs are adequate to produce a safe product. Ensures safety and potency of antibiotic drugs and insulin by requiring batch certification. Requires proof of the safety of chemicals and coloring prior to allowing them to be added to foods; requires batch certification of approved color additives. Promotes truthful labeling of foods, drugs, devices, and cosmetics, and the safe labeling of potentially hazardous consumer products. Sets limits on amount of pesticide and radioactive residues remaining on food crops that enter the market. Sets standards of identity, quality and fill-of-container for food products. Takes action to enforce the law against illegal sale or distribution of prescription drugs.

Government Printing Office: Furnishes government publications at minimum cost. About 25,000 titles are currently for sale. Sales total 65 million copies a year.

Department of the Interior: Seeks to assure adequate supplies of water for public use. Provides certain park and recreation areas and facilities for public use. Supervises facilities and services operated within the National Parks by concessionaires under contract. Markets electric power, within certain regions of the country where Federal hydroelectric power dams have been constructed. Provides protection for purchasers of Indian and Eskimo arts and crafts.

Interstate Commerce Commission: Seeks to ensure reasonable transportation charges, adequate and efficient services and public safety.

Department of Justice: Enforces Federal laws for consumer protection through cases referred to it by other Government agencies, such as FDA [Food and Drug Administration], FTC [Federal Trade Commission], Post Office, SEC [Securities and Exchange Commission]. Enforces other laws, particularly antitrust laws aimed at preventing restraints of trade and preventing mergers and other concentrations of economic power which may lead to monopolies and unfair pricing.

National Bureau of Standards (Commerce): Develops criteria with which to measure the quality and performance of materials, many of which are used in consumer goods. Sets standards for certain consumer goods and industrial materials used in making products of various types. Promotes development of uniform laws governing weights and measures.

National Traffic Safety Agency, National Highway Safety Agency (Transportation): Insure that all new cars manufactured after January 1, 1968, conform to Federal motor vehicle safety regulations. Make roads and highways safer for drivers and pedestrians. Set national standards of tests and regulations for drivers.

Office of Economic Opportunity: Helps low-income consumers learn how to get the most for their money in the purchase of goods and services. Helps low-income consumers to solve consumer problems requiring legal assistance. Improves living conditions and home-management skills of low-income persons. Provides low-income consumers with access to existing low-cost credit and savings institutions. Helps low-income consumers create their own economic institutions designed to help them solve their own community consumer problems.

Office of Renewal and Housing Assistance (HUD): Makes more low-rent housing units available for low-income persons, especially the elderly and handicapped. Helps tenants in public housing projects to improve their spending habits through consumer education. Works with manufacturers to improve household appliances and other products used in public housing projects. Seeks to improve environmental standards of neighborhoods, including better services and facilities for consumers. Helps home owners in urban renewal areas to improve their homes and ease the hardship of moving.

Post Office Department: Provides mail service. Provides insurance for valuables sent through the mails. Sells international money orders. Protects people from dangerous articles, contraband, fraudulent promotion material, and pornography transmitted by mail. Sells United States Savings Bonds.

President's Committee on Consumer Interests: Advises the President on consumer matters. Determines unmet consumer needs. Facilitates communication on consumer affairs between Government, consumers, business, states, voluntary organizations and other groups. Coordinates consumer activities of Federal agencies. Promotes consumer education. Stimulates voluntary improvements in the marketplace.

Public Health Service (HEW): Stimulates development of medical and dental facilities and public health services. Develops programs to prevent accidental injuries and control communicable and chronic diseases. Helps maintain a healthful environment by stimulating action against air pollution and other environmental health hazards. Conducts and supports health and health-related research. Aids the development of programs and facilities to train health workers. Fights mental illness through research and support for community facilities construction and mental health programs. Provides assistance to states and communities in combating epidemics and natural disasters. Guards against the introduction of communicable diseases into the United States. Provides medical services to merchant seamen, American Indians, Alaskan natives, and others eligible to receive direct Government medical services.

Rural Development and Conservation (USDA): The Service helps rural people obtain better access to Federal programs which are not now fully used in rural areas. The Farmers Home Administration provides credit and management assistance to farmers for ownership and operation of family-size farms; credit both to farm and nonfarm rural residents to build rural community water and waste disposal systems; loans for soil conservation, watershed and forestry development, and rural community recreation centers; and loans administered for the Office of Economic Opportunity to individuals and cooperatives to enable low-income rural people to earn more. The Forest Service promotes the conservation and best use of the nation's forest land resources which amount to about one third of the total land area of the United States. The Rural Electrification Administration makes loans to finance electric and telephone service for rural people. The Soil Conservation Service offers technical assistance to landowners in stabilizing and improving soil, water, plant and wildlife resources on the nation's private lands. It also helps rural landowners establish income-producing recreation areas.

Securities and Exchange Commission: Protects the public in the purchase and sale of stocks and bonds and in the operation of investment companies.

Social Security Administration (HEW): Provides an insurance program to furnish income to persons and their families in old age and in the event of disability or death. Provides a health insurance program to help pay health care expenses for persons sixty-five years of age or older. Studies problems of poverty and insecurity to see how social insurance can alleviate them.

Department of the Treasury: The Alcohol and Tobacco Tax Division or IRS [Internal Revenue Service] is charged with preventing consumer deception in the labeling and advertising of alcoholic beverages. The same division also has authority to prevent the reuse of liquor bottles and regulate other products containing alcohol. The Coast Guard is charged with protecting the safety of ship passengers and crew as well as the enforcement of Federal laws on the high seas and the navigable waters of the United States. The Secret Service guards against counterfeiting of currency, the forging of Government checks, and protects the President and Vice President. The Savings Bonds Division promotes the sale of Government bonds which provide a means of protected investment to purchasers.

The Customs Service renders services to the traveling public and the commercial community. The Bureau of Narcotics controls the import and manufacture of narcotics. The Comptroller of the Currency protects the depositors in the nation's 4,800 national banks.

Veterans Administration: For veterans only, furnishes hospitalization and other medical care. For veterans, their dependents, and their survivors, depending upon their eligibility, provides various kinds of financial benefits and other assistance.

THE TRUTH-IN-PACKAGING LEGISLATION [3]

No matter how you look at it, passage of the truth-in-packaging bill in 1966 was something of a legislative miracle. Senator Philip A. Hart [Democrat, Michigan] . . . sponsored the bill (officially titled the Fair Packaging and Labeling Act) and waged a five-year campaign to get it through Congress. . . .

The special interests fighting truth-in-packaging included food and packaging industries doing $100 billion in annual business. Acting as a united front, they put on an awesome campaign, particularly after the Senate had passed its version of the bill in June by a commanding 72-to-9 vote. Besides the usual pamphleteering and a prodigious volume of testimony given to the House Commerce Committee during the summer, they propagandized mightily in the daily press. . . .

Even after President Johnson signed the bill into law on November 3, Madison Avenue alchemized defeat into victory. William J. Colihan, Jr., a vice president of Young & Rubicam, the advertising agency, spoke for the jubilators: "Business is probably not delighted to have a bill but is probably delighted with the one they have," he said.

The truth-in-packaging law . . . certainly falls short of what it should be. Senator Warren Magnuson [Democrat, Washington], who ably steered the bill through the Senate Commerce Committee, called the final version "essentially a labeling bill." . . .

The weaknesses of the new law are plain enough when its provisions are judged against those contained in the bills that Senator

[3] From "Some Truth-in-Packaging . . . But Not Enough." *Consumer Reports.* 32:113-15. F. '67. Reprinted by permission.

Hart put in the hopper in 1962 and 1965. Senator Hart wanted Congress to require the establishment of reasonable standard weights and measures for packaged commodities so that shoppers could compare prices without having to make slide-rule calculations. Instead, Congress has called for voluntary standardization— and only when the Secretary of Commerce has, at his discretion, made a finding that a proliferation of package sizes is making price comparisons difficult.

Senator Hart wanted to prohibit "cents-off" labels on the ground —self-evident in our opinion—that manufacturers and packers cannot control either the regular retail price or the cents-off price and that, therefore, the packager promises a bargain beyond his ability to deliver. Instead, Congress has given the Food and Drug Administration and the Federal Trade Commission discretionary power to establish regulations governing cents-off and other bargain price claims.

Senator Hart wanted to prohibit pictures and illustrations on labels if they falsely depicted the contents of the package. Congress dropped that prohibition altogether.

Senator Hart wanted standards set for serving sizes so that, when a label claims a given number of servings of mashed potatoes, stew, soup, pudding, etc., the shopper will not be deceived into buying the brand falsely purporting to yield the most servings. Instead, Congress authorized the FDA to require, at its discretion, a declaration on the label giving the quantity of a serving *only* if the label specifies the number of servings. The FDA is *not* authorized to set standards.

Senator Hart wanted Congress to provide for standards for measuring the performance of products whose quantity might otherwise be misleading to a shopper making price comparisons. Liquid dishwashing detergents, for instance, might be labeled in units indicating their concentration of cleaning agent. Congress threw out the idea.

The Clean-Cut Victories

Some provisions of the new law are all that Senator Hart . . . could ask them to be. The FDA and FTC are required to set standards for the mandatory disclosure of net quantity on every package. The type size, contrasting background color, and position of the information on the label will be laid down by regulation. If the contents are less than 4 pounds or 1 gallon, quantity must be stated in total ounces as well as in pounds or quarts and their fractions if any. The shopper won't have to convert quarts or pounds to ounce of measure (32 per quart) or weight (16 per pound) in order to make price comparisons.

The new law bans once and for all the "jumbo quart" and "giant half gallon." Quantity declarations appearing in standardized form must be unadorned with qualifying adjectives. Furthermore, any word embellishing nonstandardized quantity claims elsewhere on the label will break the law if it exaggerates.

The new law authorizes the promulgation of standard words to describe different package sizes whenever the administrators find that size designations are being used deceptively or are interfering with price comparisons. FDA and FTC can, if they will, end forever the "giant" size that really is the smallest size in its line. Packages, like eggs, may have to sell themselves with well-defined versions of those old-fashioned words "small," "medium," and "large."

The new law authorizes regulations to prevent unjustifiable slack fill. That air space at the top of a box or bottle must have some function other than to cheat you. It will be permitted only if it protects the contents from being crushed, or if machinery can pack the contents no tighter (though later shipping and handling may shake them down considerably), or if the space is needed for shaking out the contents (as in household cleansers).

Every one of the reforms enumerated here has the virtue of being specific about what constitutes an economic cheat or deception. Courts will no longer have to puzzle over the intent of Congress. And that's important because court interpretations have been a major obstacle to enforcement of previous packaging regulations. As George P. Larrick, former commissioner of the FDA, testified during hearings on truth-in-packaging, his agency heretofore "lost every contested action involving deceptive packaging of food." Regulatory agencies, moreover, will no longer have to proceed case by case. They can now put the teeth of law into product-wide standards or regulations.

Declaration of Policy

If any judge has doubts about the intent of Congress, the Government need only quote the Declaration of Policy in the new law: "Informed consumers are essential to the fair and efficient functioning of a free market economy. Packages and their labels should enable consumers to obtain accurate information as to the quantity of the contents and should facilitate value comparisons. Therefore, it is hereby declared to be the policy of the Congress to assist consumers and manufacturers in reaching these goals in the marketing of consumer goods."

Those fine words notwithstanding, it is safe to predict that consumers will continue to lament, "We can't compare prices." As CU [Consumers Union of U.S., Inc., publisher of *Consumer Reports*] has said so many times, the key to effective truth-in-packaging legislation lies in setting reasonable weights and quantities. Cereals and scouring powder and paper towels, among other things, should come in at most a few standard quantities and sizes, suitable to the needs of consumers; instead, package sizes have proliferated either permanently or transitionally as the packers manipulated quantity rather than change their price.

The Role of the Secretary of Commerce

The new law merely tells the Secretary of Commerce to keep an eye out for problems, and, if he finds one, to call together a committee of manufacturers, packers, distributors and consumers to write a voluntary standard for package sizes. The Secretary has had authority to do that for many years. But his department has not, historically, championed the consumer's causes. As an administrator of truth-in-packaging, the Commerce Department strikes the National Association of Manufacturers, for one, as a strange choice "because Commerce is supposed to represent business viewpoints, and they are well aware that businessmen certainly view the Hart bill darkly."

For better or worse, the Secretary of Commerce is now Congress' consumer surrogate, with orders to follow. When the Secretary makes a finding of packaging proliferation or inability to compare prices of a household commodity, he will now be *required* to initiate standards-making. The drafters of the law, obviously familiar with the painfully slow process of getting competing and often conflicting interests to agree on a standard, wrote into the law a one-year limit on the proceedings. After the deadline, the Secretary must report to Congress, either recommending legislation to create a mandatory packaging standard or advising that no reasonable standard is possible.

The Secretary is also required to report to Congress if, a year after a voluntary standard has been established, it is not being observed. And he must make an annual report to Congress on his standards-making activities.

Despite its shortcomings, truth-in-packaging as enacted does, all in all, arm three Government agencies with sorely needed new authority over both packages and labels. Strong, consumer-oriented enforcement and administration of its provisions *can* turn those 6000 to 8000 packaged salesmen along the supermarket aisles into information purveyors of a useful sort. [As of mid-1968 the Federal agencies have done a very minimum necessary to bring this to pass. —The Author.]

THE TRUTH-IN-LENDING LEGISLATION [4]

Senate passage of the truth-in-lending bill last July [1967] represented a 92-to-0 vote of confidence in the ability of consumers to shop wisely for credit when given the essential facts. Those facts concern the true price of money, whether borrowed directly from a lending institution or indirectly through the purchase of goods and services on the installment plan.

Except in the realm of consumer credit, the price of money is everywhere expressed as an annual interest rate—the percentage of principal the borrower must pay for a year's use of someone else's

[4] From "The Big Hole in Truth-in-Lending." *Consumer Reports.* 32:470-4. S. '67. Reprinted by permission.

money. Truth-in-lending legislation would simply give consumers the same information that has always formed the basis for non-consumer borrowing. For the first time in the history of this buy-now-pay-later economy, consumers would be able to make accurate price comparisons in shopping for most types of credit. The one major exception—and it could easily become a gaping hole in the dike—is revolving credit.

The Relative Truth

The marked differential between the true annual interest rate and the actual number of dollars charged per $100 of initial install-ment credit has long been a source of hopeless confusion. A "price" of $6 for $100 of credit, to be repaid in 12 monthly installments, is not equivalent to an annual interest rate of 6 per cent. It *would* be 6 per cent if you kept the whole $100 for a full year and repaid it in one lump sum. But you usually repay it in regular installments, and thereby lose the use of a progressively larger fraction of $100 during the year.

The true annual installment interest rate is thus usually about twice the dollars-per-hundred figure. If you borrow $100 for one year and pay back $106 in equal monthly installments, the true annual rate is not 6 per cent but 10.9 per cent. If you borrow $100, immediately pay $6 interest, and pay off $100 in one year's install-ments, the rate is 11.6 per cent.

Defining the annual interest rate on consumer credit is the Senate's major contribution to truth-in-lending. Truth, in lending as in everything else, is relative, and writing the definition of true annual interest has not been an easy exercise in standards-making. Several different ways of calculating installment interest rates have been in common use. Each produces a somewhat different rate from the same set of terms, because each makes a different assumption about how the interest is being paid. For example, does all the in-terest come out of the first payment? Does it all come out of the final payment? Is it divided equally among all payments? Is it a decreasing portion of each payment?

In recent editions of the Buying Guide Issue of *Consumer Reports,* we have published an equation for calculating annual interest. It is based on the constant-ratio method— each payment is assumed to consist of a fixed portion of interest and principal, equaling the total of each divided by the number of installments. Most credit sellers, it turns out, use another method giving slightly different rates. It is a decreasing-interest method, which applies the interest rate each month to the unpaid balance. This method has been explained simply and clearly in the "Financial Rate Translater," a publication of rate tables for use by the credit industry:

Traditionally the return on money invested is stated as an annual interest rate on the funds actually in use. For monthly payment loans the interest rate per month is $1/_{12}$ of the annual interest rate. In these tables we shall call this *annual* interest rate the *actuarial* rate. It is exactly the same rate you talk about for a GI mortgage, or an FHA mortgage or any other direct reduction loan. *The actuarial rate expresses the true return on an investment; any other is at best an approximation.*

The last sentence, which we have emphasized, tells the story. From the consumer's view, the lender's true (gross) return equals the true annual interest rate.

The Senate has taken its definition straight from the horse's mouth. Its draft of the bill calls for use of the actuarial method, and would instruct the Federal Reserve Board to describe methods for computing actuarial interest rates for almost any conceivable installment credit arrangement now in common use. Credit contracts would have to state, additionally, the rest of the payment terms: the purchase price, the size of the down payment, the balance to be financed as a loan, the number, size and frequency of payments and the total finance charge. Some states already require disclosure of some or all of those items. Only one, Massachusetts, requires disclosure of the annual interest rate (as figured by the constant-ratio method).

There is every indication that the House of Representatives will also pass a truth-in-lending bill. [It did, and President Johnson signed the bill, putting the full force of his influence behind compulsory disclosure of true annual interest.—Ed.]

Legislative Purpose

The strengths and weaknesses of the bill . . . can be properly understood only in terms of the purposes underlying it. To be sure, politicians are as much in favor of truth as they are against sin. But truth as such is not the basic objective. Behind . . . the truth-in-lending bill is a vital need for marketing tools to help stabilize a most turbulent sector of the national economy.

Total short-term consumer debt has been growing at a furious pace. In the past fifteen years, it has quadrupled to a present level of around $95 billion. About $75 billion is installment debt, on which repayments last year were $73 billion. By comparison, total personal income has only a little more than doubled in the same fifteen years, and now stands at about $505 billion, after taxes. Plain arithmetic thus says that about every seventh dollar in the average pay envelope is spent before it's earned.

And plain arithmetic understates the case. You must add interest charges of about $12.5 billion per year. You must also take into account that only about half of the nation's wage earners have short-term installment debts. Installment debt alone, plus its interest, is generally estimated as laying prior claim to one dollar of every four in an *average debtor's* pay.

Some economists fear that, with so large a part of future income committed in advance, any serious rise in unemployment or drop in wages would snowball into a major recession. For many people would have all they could do to make their payments; they would be in no position to increase their debts, and their cash buying power would be harshly curtailed. Nevertheless, the present long-term economic boom has been stimulated by the huge and expanding wave of consumer credit. It is therefore understandable that nobody in the Government has come out against the fast-growing consumer installment debt as such.

It's the turbulent fluctuations in credit expansion that cause official concern. Like Robert Louis Stevenson's little shadow, the rate of increase in consumer credit sometimes shoots up taller like an India-rubber ball, and sometimes gets so little that there's none of it at all. The pattern of sharp rises and falls over the past fifteen years . . . [reveals] three periods of extraordinary credit growth. After the first two peaks, in 1955 and 1959, the rate of borrowing fell to around the break-even point, where, over a year's time, the total of new borrowing very nearly equaled the total of repayments.

Do purchasing *intentions* normally fluctuate so wildly? Or does some outside force radically change them?

Looking back from the vantage point of the recession year 1958, CU saw signs of the lender's hand at work. "Seven million high-priced autos were moved out of dealers' inventories [in 1955] in one of the biggest sales blitzes of all time," we noted, "and some 60 per cent or better of those cars were sold on the cuff. Moreover, one of the tools of the blitz was an extension of installment contracts to thirty-six months. Other sellers, competing with autos for their share of the consumer dollars, also offered terms of nothing down and thirty-six months to pay for rugs, furniture, etc."

The chief symptom of recession is a slackening of economic growth. Thus, in 1958 there was no increase in the Gross National Product. Credit expansion hit another new high in 1959, followed by almost no credit expansion in 1961. Again, the trough on the graph was accompanied by a sharp tapering off of economic growth. To put it mildly, more orderly use of credit might have a less unsettling effect on the general economy. . . .

Underlying full disclosure of credit costs is a two-part theory to which CU has long subscribed. First, disclosure of true annual interest rates will make people more sensitive to the high price they pay for most installment loans. When 800 CU members reported a few years ago to the National Bureau of Economic Research on recent credit deals, only a minority of them said they had any idea of the interest rate they had paid. Within that minority, the average rate they *thought* they had paid was about 8 per cent. The rate they had actually paid averaged about 23 per cent (*Consumer Reports*, October 1964).

The second part of the theory holds that people who are conscious of the price of credit will shop, compare and buy that credit at as low a rate as they can find. Again, the data obtained from CU members accords with the theory. Those who were able to report the true rate of interest on their loans paid an average, for loans of under $500, of about 12 per cent. Those who had no idea of the rate paid a startling average of about 37 per cent.

In its report on the truth-in-lending bill, the Senate Banking and Currency Committee took cognizance of that and other evidence. The Senate's vote of confidence in the consumer says, in so many words, "Here is the information you need. Now don't make waves." . . .

Special Treatment for Revolving Credit

When it became quite evident . . . that some kind of truth-in-lending bill would be passed, one of its old-line opponents, the National Retail Merchants Association, sent out this advisory to its members: "With . . . the prospect of more intensive pressures for credit controls during 1967, it is becoming increasingly evident that flat opposition to credit legislation may be doomed to failure. *A wiser course might be to work for legislation and regulations that can be lived with.*" (Italics supplied by the NRMA.)

At Senate hearings . . . witnesses for the NRMA and a number of other strong opponents of the bill concentrated their fire on one provision in particular. They sought to knock out any requirement for annual rate disclosure on revolving credit charge accounts. And they largely succeeded. Under the Senate bill, revolving credit as applied to most department store accounts and most of the new wave of revolving bank credit cards would continue to be labeled, as it usually is now, with a deceptively low monthly percentage figure.

Revolving credit is one kind of consumer credit most people are familiar with, whether or not they make a practice of buying on time. People who buy at all regularly in most department stores or from big mail order houses usually open charge accounts. It's convenient to pay the bill once a month, and, besides, there's usually no credit charge if you pay the bill within thirty days. Every customer, whether he pays cash over the counter or says charge it, foots the costs of thirty-day credit as part of the overhead built into the price of the goods.

Of course, most stores offer a choice of paying in full or making a payment of, usually, 10 per cent per month. It's what's called a "line of credit" or an "open-end" credit account. Each new purchase is added to the bill, and 10 per cent of the total balance at the end of each billing period is all you have to pay ad infinitum—all, that is, except for a "small" monthly service charge. Many states set a service charge ceiling of $1\frac{1}{2}$ per cent per month, and stores almost invariably charge the maximum. A rate of $1\frac{1}{2}$ per cent a month equals an annual interest rate of $1\frac{1}{2}$ times 12, or 18 per cent.

The balance due on the nation's charge accounts has been running at $10.5 billion. About $3.5 billion is revolving credit. That's not much next to the total installment credit outstanding. But it is probably not an accurate figure at present, and it certainly won't be an accurate one in the future, because it omits, among other things, the revolving credit schemes now being heavily merchandised by banks. Until last year, bank revolving credit was probably not a major factor, although it has been on the scene at least since 1950. But in only the past year or two, according to the Federal Reserve Board, the number of banks issuing credit cards or operating open-end check credit plans reached 627, plus several hundred local banks acting as agents for large city banks' credit plans.

"The enthusiasm with which the supposedly conservative banking profession has greeted this relatively new consumer service is unparalleled in the pages of modern banking history," the American Bankers Association was told by a Chicago banker. And he explained why: "We are beginning with this first step to recapture a larger share of the credit business which heretofore conceivably could have fallen into nonbanking hands by default."

The bank credit card, unlike the department store card, can be used to charge purchases at many different stores—as many as can be recruited by the sponsoring bank. It is the poor man's version of the American Express or Diners' Club card. As *The Wall Street Journal* has reported, "Bank cards are issued largely to lower-income consumers. . . ." A number of Midwest banks, operating jointly, "mailed mounds of credit cards unsolicited to each other's customers and former customers, some four million families in all," the *Journal* said. . . .

Were the final truth-in-lending law to exempt bank, department store and mail-order charge accounts from annual rate disclosure, it would quite obviously withhold from the consumer an important tool he needs to shop wisely for credit. Yet the Senate bill exempts those accounts, in most instances.

If the exemption is allowed to stand, only the monthly rate will be disclosed on most revolving credit deals. To compare the price of revolving credit with that of other forms of credit you would have to convert the monthly rate to an annual rate by multiplying it by twelve. Many people don't know that, however, and they might assume that a $1\frac{1}{2}$ per cent service charge is lower than, say, the 12 per cent annual rate generally charged by credit unions. There is thus some likelihood that the exemption would help accelerate the growth of revolving credit.

To escape annual rate disclosure for revolving credit, merchants and bankers used a shrewd argument on the Senate subcommittee considering truth-in-lending. A charge account customer, they said, often gets the use of their money at $1\frac{1}{2}$ per cent for more than one month. Someone who buys something shortly after his monthly bill has been made out, for instance, would have as long as 59 days of free time before incurring a service charge, because he would not receive his next bill, with the new item posted on it, for up to 29 days and would have 30 additional days after that to pay it. Therefore, the argument goes, a $1\frac{1}{2}$ per cent service charge does not accurately translate as 18 per cent per annum and is usually lower.

The argument has a cute premise: Up to 59 days of credit time are available interest-free, but only on condition that the bill is paid in full on the 59th day. (In practice, you'd better pay it sooner or it might not be credited to your account in time to escape interest.) If you don't pay in full, time runs backward to the date of purchase.

Well, maybe an accountant can really make the calendar run in reverse. But one name for that sort of magic is account juggling.

The only reason for mentioning it here is that there are many different sets of rules for juggling revolving credit. Different stores use different rules, and they are not just playing games. A revolving charge account can cost considerably more at one store or bank than another, though both seem to be charging 18 per cent annual interest.

Professor Richard L. D. Morse of Kansas State University has illustrated the situation dramatically in a recent pamphlet. He demonstrates six different revolving credit billing systems, all of them examples of systems in use, and he showed how service charges can run more than twice as high in some stores as in others. . . .

The point, of course, is that hardly anyone can fathom the billing methods of revolving charge accounts. Help is needed, and the need will become more and more pressing as banks and stores, spurred on by the availability of computerized billing systems, contend for revolving credit business.

[A new truth-in-lending bill was signed into law on May 29, 1968. It is designed to give consumers full and clear information on how much they pay in interest and other charges on loans and credit purchases. Finance companies, banks, other lenders, and retailers will be required to inform borrowers and credit customers of credit charges in terms of annual percentage rates on the declining balance of obligations, with few exceptions. They will also have to inform borrowers of the dollars-and-cents cost of financing loans and purchases. The bill includes a special rule for "revolving" charge accounts, requiring that both monthly and annual interest rates on such accounts must be stated unless they amount to less than 50 cents a month and are billed as service charges. The new truth-in-lending bill is officially titled the Consumer Credit Protection Act.—Ed.]

CONTROLLING DECEPTIVE ADVERTISING [5]

Deceptive advertising has afflicted American commerce from the time advertising began to gain momentum in early American newspapers. The worst abuses were instigated by the manufacturers of patent medicines. . . .

[5] From *FTC and Deceptive Advertising,* by Max L. Marshall, part-time instructor at the School of Journalism, University of Missouri. (Freedom of Information Center Report no. 183) University of Missouri. School of Journalism. Columbia. '67. Reprinted by permission.

Early Attempts to Limit Malpractices

Destined to eventually achieve some measure of success in reducing advertising malpractice, however, were the efforts made by *Printers' Ink*. Begun as a promotion organ for the George P. Rowell advertising agency and ear-marked to become a foremost twentieth century trade journal, *Printers' Ink* in 1911 formulated the famed "model statute," which was soon adopted as law by a number of states. It made untruthful, deceptive or misleading statements by an advertiser punishable as a misdemeanor.

Another forward step was taken in 1915, when the Associated Advertising Clubs of America established the National Vigilance Committee. It too was aimed at reducing dishonest advertising, and this positive force would later become known as the Better Business Bureau (BBB). [See "The Role of Better Business Bureaus" in Section III, below.—Ed.]

A year earlier, an important landmark was reached when Congress passed the Federal Trade Commission Act creating the Federal Trade Commission (FTC). Unrecognized at the time was the tremendous power this new agency would eventually wield. In its original form, the law was primarily aimed at controlling unfair competition in restraint of trade and enforcing the antitrust laws. Before long, however, the FTC would become the nation's most dominant force in checking advertising malfeasance.

Meanwhile efforts continued within the private sector, and advertising codes and guidelines began to proliferate. The Association of National Advertisers (ANA) cooperating with the American Association of Advertising Agencies (AAAA) sponsored a joint code of ethics in 1932, in a self-regulatory effort to control false or misleading advertising; subsequently a Review Committee was established in hopes of providing means of enforcement.

The AAAA has acted in other ways. It promulgated a "Creative Code" in 1962 acknowledging industry's responsibility to both advertiser and the consumer. Again, guidelines were spelled out and enforcement procedures attempted.

Related codes of ethics and self-regulatory efforts have mushroomed in recent years. The Advertising Federation of America

(AFA), concerned with advertising carried over local media, has set down its own version. The Direct Mail Advertising Association has spelled out guidelines; the National Association of Broadcasters (NAB) has published an extensive ethical code in its NAB Seal of Good Practice; this is supplemented by those of individual broadcasting associations. The American Newspaper Publishers' Association (ANPA) has addressed itself to the problem in more general terms.

Different industries in the United States have likewise been active. There is the Revised Advertising Code for the Film Industry, established by the Motion Picture Association of America. The Magazine Publishers' Association has a Copy Advisory Committee. Codes sponsored by nonmedia industries seldom come to the notice of the general public. Typical among these are those established by such associations as the National Tire Retreaders Association, or the Air Transport Association.

Local municipal organizations also concern themselves with the quality of advertising. The Miami Advertising Code and Code Committee and the Cleveland Plan for Maintaining Public Confidence in Advertising are two examples. The latter has been widely copied by municipalities across the nation. . . .

Governmental Controls of Deceptive Advertising

Self-regulation in the private sector of the economy is but one side of the coin. Governmental controls of advertising are the other. These are many and varied, with one agency—the Federal Trade Commission—predominant. As the legally appointed sentry of deceptive advertising practices, it probably wields more power and influence than all other agencies, both private and public, combined. This is not to derogate the controls exercised by other Federal organizations. They are potent and vigorous. But across-the-board control of advertising malfeasance is a "specialty" of the FTC whereas in other agencies, it is either a sideline or else confined to a very narrow sector.

For example, the *labeling* authority of the Food and Drug Administration often brings its functions close to the areas in which the FTC exercises responsibility (the law gives the FTC specific enforcement authority in matters of misleading advertising of foods or proprietary drugs). An agreement has been worked out between the two agencies to prevent overlapping and duplication.

The Post Office Department can act in matters pertaining to lotteries, fraud, or obscenity; it has power to refuse mail delivery— or almost as devastating from a financial standpoint in applicable cases, the ability to withdraw second class mailing privileges. In certain instances it is empowered to stamp the word "fraudulent" on the outside of envelopes. When more drastic action is deemed necessary, it can prosecute under appropriate criminal statutes.

While the Federal Communications Commission (FCC) has no such direct weapons, it is nevertheless concerned with advertising that is obscene, profane, fraudulent or deceptive. Broadcasters are fully aware of the FCC's indirect powers stemming from its broad licensing authority. Disaster can overtake anyone who, in the opinion of the FCC, fails to operate in the "public interest." Even an FCC-administered slap on the wrist for a minor infraction can sting. Administered by the simple expedient of granting only a temporary one-year license extension rather than the regular three-year renewal, it results in substantial financial outlays in legal fees and other costs, to say nothing of the anxiety involved.

The Securities and Exchange Act of 1934 empowers the Securities and Exchange Commission (SEC) to regulate the sale and issuance of securities. Thus the SEC plays a dominant role in controlling advertising deception in this specific area. The Bureau of Internal Revenue, too, is involved in advertising regulation. Its Alcohol Tax Unit has supervisory powers over matters relating to the advertising of alcoholic beverages. A veritable jungle of controls is entered when one considers the different state laws concerned with advertising regulation. They are so varied and complicated that no attempt can be made to describe them in this paper.

This then is the environmental structure within which, and over which, the FTC pursues its functions. How are the activities of the FTC carried out? To what extent is its work effective? How has the Commission developed, and what specific things has it been doing in recent years? These are the questions to which this paper is addressed.

Organization and Background

The FTC's well-publicized activities in the control of false and misleading advertising have led many elements of the general public to overlook the fact that the Commission was originally created to combat concentrations of excessive economic power accumulated by great trusts and monopolies before and around the turn of the twentieth century. Also often overlooked is the fact that the FTC has many other functions and is responsible for the enforcement of numerous public laws.

At the very top of the FTC pyramid, the Commission is composed of five members, appointed by the President and confirmed by the Senate for terms of seven years. The President also appoints the chairman.

The official manual of the Federal Trade Commission *(Organization, Procedures, Rules of Practice, and Statutes)* assigns the responsibility for controls over false and misleading advertising to the Bureau of Deceptive Practices. This top echelon Bureau—on a par with such others as the one exercising responsibility over matters concerning restraint of trade—is itself divided into five major divisions: Food and Drug Advertising; General Practices (jurisdiction over allegedly deceptive practices in selling all products other than food and drugs); Special Projects (makes studies and has other broad assignments in special consumer protection areas); Division of Compliance (charged with enforcement); and the Division of Scientific Opinions. This last division was created to furnish advice, information and assistance to the staff regarding the "composition, nature, effectiveness, and safety of food, drugs, devices, cosmetics and related commodities."

The current organization has jelled over a period of time and the FTC's effectiveness in the realm of misleading advertising is largely derived from the fact that over the years expertise derived from long experience, combined with legislative enactments and court rulings, have put some very sharp teeth into FTC regulatory and enforcement procedures. . . .

FTC "Ground Rules"

To understand the manner in which the FTC seeks to control deceptive advertising, it is necessary to be familiar with the "basic ground rules," as set forth by former FTC Chairman Earl W. Kintner. These rules are followed not only by the FTC, but the principles they incorporate have been widely adopted in advertising codes promulgated by the private sector of the U.S. economy. There are six in number:

1. *Tendency to deceive.* The Commission is empowered to act when representations have only a *tendency* to mislead or deceive. Proof of *actual* deception is not essential, although evidence of actual deception is apparently conclusive as to the deceptive quality of the advertisement in question.

2. *Immateriality of knowledge of falsity.* Since the purpose of the FTC act is consumer protection, the Government does not have to prove knowledge of falsity on the part of the advertiser; the businessman acts at his own peril.

3. *Immateriality of intent.* The intent of the advertiser is also entirely immaterial. An advertiser may have a wholly innocent intent and still violate the law.

4. *General public's understanding controls.* Since the purpose of the act is to protect the consumers, and since some consumers are "ignorant, unthinking and credulous," nothing less than "the most literal truthfulness" is tolerated. As the Supreme Court has stated, "laws are made to protect the trusting as well as the suspicious." Thus it is immaterial that an expert reader might be able to decipher the advertisement in question so as to avoid being misled.

5. *Literal truth sometimes insufficient.* Advertisements are not intended to be carefully dissected with a dictionary at hand, but rather are intended to produce an over-all impression on the ordinary purchaser. An advertiser cannot present one over-all impression and yet protect himself by pointing to a contrary impression which appears in a small and inconspicuous portion of the advertisement. Even though every sentence considered separately is true, the advertise-

ment as a whole may be misleading because the message is composed in such a way as to mislead.

6. *Ambiguous advertisements interpreted to effect purposes of the law.* Since the purpose of the FTC Act is the prohibition of advertising which has a tendency and capacity to mislead, an advertisement which can be read to have two meanings is illegal if one of them is false or misleading.

In order to translate these ground rules into effective action, the FTC engages in a two-pronged attack. It conducts a broad "educational" program designed to guide industries and organizations—to explain the laws and to obtain voluntary compliance. And it takes action against individual violators....

Reactions to FTC Practices

Generally speaking, commentary on Federal Trade Commission actions relating to control of deceptive advertising has been most favorable. Professor Milton Handler, in the Introduction to the Symposium on the Fiftieth Anniversary of the Federal Trade Commission, praised these activities in the following terms: "Through its outlawing of unfair and deceptive acts, the Commission has rendered yeoman service in raising the plane of competition." He continues, "It is here that the Commission has made its most notable contributions to substantive doctrine.

The people, through their elected representatives in Congress, have affirmed their belief in the value of FTC services; this has been evidenced by the increasing increments of authority voted to the FTC. Judging from support rendered by past and current Administrations, the Executive, too, has approved the manner in which this work has been performed.

The courts also have given solid support to the FTC in most advertising deception cases. In fact, a review of the three most recent annual reports of the Federal Trade Commission reveals that the Commission has prevailed in an extremely high proportion of cases brought to court—almost invariably, in fact. These same annual reports would also indicate that the Commission maintains a well-oiled and effective legal machinery with which to deal routinely with disputes which come up for judicial decision. It would seem that the word "dismissed" is seldom the last one.

A lawyer and scholar of the stature of Glen E. Weston, who has studied intensively in the area of FTC practices, has said: "Unlike the controversial antitrust and Robinson-Patman jurisdiction, the Federal Trade Commission's false advertising work has been almost universally recognized as having significant value." Moreover, he points out that though less than half the Commission's appropriations have been spent for this purpose, "it was here that the greatest achievements were being made." He cites some additional impressive facts: "It (the Commission) has issued several thousand complaints and cease-and-desist orders, has accepted over twelve thousand formal stipulations to cease particular practices, has obtained countless informal assurances of discontinuance of false advertising claims and has screened or monitored millions of advertisements."

There is more. In describing Commission accomplishments in industry-wide actions, Weston points out that the FTC "has formulated Trade Practice Conference Rules for more than 160 industries, has published eleven sets of Advertising Guides, and has issued new trade regulation rules for seven industries."

Fairfax M. Cone, president of Foote, Cone & Belding, and past chairman of the American Association of Advertising Agencies, also credits the Commission with performing a worth-while service in controlling deceptive advertising practices. In a speech titled "Advertising and the Market Place" delivered at the Ninth Annual Freedom of Information Conference at the School of Journalism, University of Missouri (December 5, 1966), Mr. Cone stated that though most advertising is honest, recourse can be had in instances of misleading or deceptive practices. He even went so far as to advocate more funds for the FTC (and other agencies) with which to enlarge such activities. He said:

I would be a fool not to know that there are dishonest people in business and in advertising, or that they play on the emotions of emotional people in businesses where sales are made to once-in-a-lifetime purchasers and there is little redress. Fortunately, as I have noted, we have the

Federal Trade Commission and the Food and Drug Administration to protect against the depredation of the first of these, and the Better Business Bureaus to move against the second. All three could do more with more funds, and I trust they will have these—mostly to discover humbuggery at the outset, and to prosecute the perpetrators with dispatch.

Certainly no champion of governmental controls in business matters, Mr. Cone made these remarks in the course of a ringing denunciation of further governmental intervention in the marketplace.

Comments and Conclusions

In sum, it would appear that in doing its daily job of policing advertising deception, the Federal Trade Commission has usually acted judiciously, wisely and effectively—and that its efforts have met with almost universal approval.

But this atmosphere of general approval does not prevail with regard to FTC advertising controls which go beyond the "Thou shalt not" dictate—and which extend into the "Thou shalt!" area. There is a definite trend in this direction which so far has been supported by the courts.

While the Supreme Court has become increasingly liberal in matters pertaining to the constitutional rights of individuals—for example, obscenity determinations are now based on whether the questionable materials appeal to the prurient interest of the *average* man—the courts have tended to back the FTC in protecting, not the *average consumer,* but the "helpless," ignorant or uneducated one.

This may be part of the rationale which has led the Commission to move forward from its base territory of controlling deceptive, false, or otherwise misleading advertising, and to proceed against advertising which "confuses." In this category might fall such guides as those which call for the "proper" labeling of products—tires, for example. The words "informative advertising" are increasingly heard. Some businessmen fear that a definite shift toward positive governmental controls over advertising is in prospect.

That such fears are not entirely groundless can be inferred from a recent United Press International article (June 6, 1967). It reported that the Commission was again appealing to Congress for stringent legislation to control cigarette advertising. In this instance, the FTC has no specific charges to make in connection with advertising statements considered to be false or misleading. Instead, the Commission objected to the "barrage of commercials on television, which portray smoking as a harmless and enjoyable social activity that is not habit-forming and involves no hazards to health."

Even more objectionable to certain business interests is the controversy concerning whether the major advertisers inhibit competition and encourage monopoly. The recent Supreme Court ruling which directed Procter & Gamble to sell off Clorox came about after the FTC invoked its powers relating to antitrust and advertising regulation. . . . Should this incident develop into a trend—or should maximum advertising dollar expenditures be set—the FTC will have taken a larger step in the direction of expanded activities into new and controversial territory.

REGULATING DRUG ADVERTISEMENTS [6]

The Government made public . . . [in May 1967] new regulations on the advertising of prescription drugs that, in effect, tell advertisers to claim nothing for their products that cannot be supported by substantial evidence.

The regulations by the Food and Drug Administration list thirty-four practices that would cause the agency to classify an advertisement as "false, lacking in fair balance or otherwise misleading."

These include any assertion in an advertisement that a drug is better, safer, more effective or has fewer side effects than has been demonstrated by medical evidence.

The regulations apply only to the advertising and labeling of prescription drugs, most often advertised in medical publications. Advertising for over-the-counter nonprescription drugs sold generally to the public at drug stores is regulated by the Federal Trade Commission.

[6] From "F.D.A. Toughens Regulations for Ads on Prescription Drugs." *New York Times.* p 57. My. 22, '67. © 1967 by The New York Times Company. Reprinted by permission.

Staff Reviewed Ads

The drug agency said the revised list of advertising practices was based on the observations of staff members who reviewed a number of published advertisements. No companies or advertising agencies are named in the regulations, which were made available at the request of the drug industry.

The Federal Drug Administration has been waging a campaign against misleading advertising and drug claims . . . and has brought a number of suits against companies it believes have advertised improperly.

"Industry representatives have asked for clarification of the regulations that have been in effect since 1963," Commissioner James L. Goddard said in a statement. "The revisions we are proposing today will provide the most precise guidelines that have been requested."

The revised regulations warn against:

Claiming advantages for a drug without simultaneously disclosing any pertinent disadvantages

Failing to present information concerning side effects and contraindications in as much depth and detail as claims for effectiveness or safety

Using favorable information or opinions that have been rendered obsolete by contrary and more recent information

Using animal data in a way that suggests they represent clinical studies

Using apparently favorable statements from recognized authorities while omitting unfavorable data or statements from the same authority

Using a quote or paraphrase out of context to convey a false or misleading idea. . . .

History of Guidelines

The new advertising guidelines stem from amendments enacted in 1962 to the Pure Food, Drug and Cosmetic Act, after an investigation led by the late Senator Estes Kefauver.

These amendments gave the drug agency, among other things, increased power to control the advertising of drugs. It has only been within the last year, however, that the agency has chosen to exercise its added powers.

After Dr. Goddard became the agency's commissioner on January 17, 1966, he warned the drug houses of rising pressures to bring the industry under tighter Federal control unless the pharmaceutical makers put their own house in order.

Dr. Goddard specifically condemned advertising that exaggerated a drug's effect and made "emotional appeals," instead of scientific ones, for its use.

The pharmaceutical manufacturers and their advertising agencies retorted that the existing rules were vague and unspecific and called for more definite rulings. . . . [The present] action was the result.

[Dr. James L. Goddard, Commissioner of Food and Drugs, resigned his post on May 21, 1968.—Ed.]

CONTROLLING FOOD PRODUCTS [7]

Tough-talking Food and Drug Commissioner James Goddard, after battling bitterly with the drug makers, is adopting a far softer approach toward the nation's food companies. He's stressing partnership, not punishment.

Instead of clamping down with seizures and court actions against products deemed unsafe, Dr. Goddard is encouraging the food processors to police the purity of their production themselves, but under the wary eye of the Food and Drug Administration. His aim is to increase consumer protection and lower the Government's regulatory costs, though some consumer and industry spokesmen fear the result will be just the opposite.

So far, this self-regulation strategy is getting a tryout with only a single company, General Foods Corporation, at only one plant, in Dover, Delaware, and on only two products, Jello-O gelatin desserts and Jell-O Golden Egg Custard Mix. But this one arrangement

[7] From "Soft-Treatment for Jell-O: Self-Regulation of Food Products' Purity by Processors Is Aim of New FDA Project," by Jonathan Spivak, staff reporter. *Wall Street Journal*. p 26. N. 24, '67. Reprinted by permission.

could signal a broad turnabout in the agency's consumer-protection techniques. If it works the FDA intends to extend it throughout the food industry and then perhaps to cosmetic and drug concerns as well.

Steps Set Jointly

In the new approach, known as self-certification, FDA and company officials sit down together and establish: (1) specific contamination limits to assure the manufacture of safe products; (2) company quality-control tests and other inspections to insure these standards are met; (3) a reporting system to make certain that the FDA learns promptly of any company shortcomings and the corrective steps taken.

In essence, the arrangement gives the FDA access to quality-control records and other information the industry has long refused to divulge, while freeing cooperating food companies from the threat of periodic Government inspections. Officials reason that the agency has insufficient staff (800 inspectors) to police thoroughly food, drug and cosmetic manufacturers with total sales above $100 billion a year; by switching the burden of inspection to companies willing to assume responsibility, the FDA can gain a continuous check on their product quality and focus its regulatory force against marginal operators.

But consumer spokesmen worry that self-certification may lead the agency to become too friendly with an industry it must police. "I've always been a little bit uncomfortable about self-regulation: I don't like it as a substitute for inspection," declares Ann Draper, an AFL-CIO research associate and a member of the FDA's Citizen Advisory Committee. "I'm not wholly convinced you wouldn't need a good watchdog on this."

Some industry men are critical of the plan, for opposite reasons: They fear it will be used to extend Government regulation unnecessarily. "Does the FDA have in mind less inspection, less cost to the taxpayer?" asks Frank Lawler, editor of the trade publication *Food Engineering.* "Or does it mean to use this as a way to dig deeper into the industry—another way to get some of the industry's secrets, some of their proprietary formulas?"...

What's new in the whole program is moving within the plant the concept of protection, which FDA has historically conceived of as seizing the product in commerce outside the plant [declares Assistant FDA Commissioner Edward Tuerk]. We want to assure that the probability is minimal of defective products going into commerce and to give industry a chance to upgrade the level of control.

Furthermore, officials recognize that many food-contamination problems, such as the spread of salmonella and other infectious organisms, can't be detected by conventional Government examination of factory-production processes, but require complex laboratory analysis of samples. And the FDA's own laboratories aren't as large as those of a single major manufacturer, such as General Foods.

New Knowledge Seen

"We'd actually be more knowledgeable as a result of this kind of program being implemented," insists Dr. Goddard. "We'd know why a batch was reworked or discarded. This might point to a specific kind of problem in a production facility we weren't even aware of."

Self-certification is starting in the food industry, rather than in drugs or cosmetics, for several reasons. Food manufacturers constitute the FDA's largest regulatory burden; they operate more than thirty thousand plants. Many food companies, dependent on constant consumer satisfaction, already enforce high standards of quality control and would presumably be quite willing to cooperate with the agency. And it may be that the food industry, with a generally high reputation for purity of product, could effectively resist a tougher, more punitive approach by the FDA. . . .

The plan is starting with a one-year trial; sooner or later it will apply to all seventeen items manufactured at the Dover plant, including Baker's chocolate and coconut products and Log Cabin syrup. For the present, the company has agreed it won't advertise its participation in the project. Nor will the FDA relinquish its rights to proceed against the company if adulterated products should turn up in the marketplace.

But the arrangement does offer General Foods important advantages. The precise anticontamination standards it spells out will, if met, assure the company of marketing a legally acceptable product. Limiting the risk of product recalls or seizures by the FDA gives the company an important economic and public-relations advantage.

If the year's trial goes well, the FDA will probably permit General Foods to publicize the fact that its products are manufactured under exacting Government-approved self-certification standards. Such claims could influence the food-buying decisions of Federal, state and other purchasing agents as well as those of individual consumers. Eventually, the FDA might even approve an official seal of sorts for consumer packages, though only if self-certification spread widely through the food industry; should the pilot project succeed, the FDA will selectively invite other companies to participate.

For the FDA, the self-certification tryout offers an opportunity to determine, with suitable safeguards, just how far it can rely on a manufacturer's sense of public responsibility. The agency currently keeps aloof from the food companies. If Federal regulators find fault during a plant inspection, the company usually learns about it later through formal legal action. There has been little attempt to establish Federal standards to help companies produce acceptable products, and there has been infrequent exchange of information between the industry and the FDA about consumer protection.

Under the new approach, the agency and General Foods first established specific product standards designed to protect the public against both health hazards and economic deception.

[Dr. James L. Goddard, Commissioner of Food and Drugs, resigned his post on May 21, 1968.—Ed.]

PROTECTING MAIL ORDER CONSUMERS [8]

In all the publicity emanating from Washington, D.C., setting forth the consumer protection activities of various bureaus, depart-

[8] From "The Post Office Protects Consumers Against Fraud." *Consumer Bulletin.* 50:19-20. N. '67. Reprinted by permission of Consumer Bulletin, Washington, N.J. 07882. Copyright 1967.

ments, and agencies, very little notice has been taken of the unobtrusive but effective work of Postal Inspection Service, Fraud and Mailability Section, of the United States Post Office. Mail-order advertising that misrepresents merchandise, vendors' failure to deliver merchandise ordered through the mail, collecting payment for magazines that are never delivered are just a few of the many cases handled by the Postal Inspection Service. . . .

Currently, the Postal Inspection Service has stepped up its attack on chain-referral schemes, which are often centered around appliances such as vacuum cleaners sold at exorbitant prices. In August 1967, it was reported that the Post Office was investigating 109 such plans. One frequently used deal involves the sale of a vacuum cleaner priced at something like $250. The unlucky victim is persuaded to sign his name to a paper that commits him to make regular payments by a persuasive pitch that all he needs do is make a $19.90 down payment. Then he can easily handle the balance by persuading his friends to buy this wonderful cleaner and for each friend to whom the salesman is enabled to make a sale, he will receive a $25 credit against his own purchase. Some of these schemes carry the chain referral a step farther. Each prospect must also bring in ten more (and so on) for the first victim to get his refund or credit.

Now . . . an efficient vacuum cleaner can be obtained for $50 to $100, depending on the type desired. In one particular case in which the Government has secured an indictment, the salesmen had not revealed that the purchaser to get the vacuum cleaner at a modest price would have to find ten additional buyers. Actually, the Government reported, only 10 per cent of the families buying the high-priced vacuum cleaner received more than three bonuses or $75. Even at that, the cleaner they signed up for was far from being a bargain. . . .

Another mail-order promotion which has been subject to postal fraud action by Federal authorities is a device called Unitron claimed to produce "gas-savings as high as 34 per cent" as reported by "University Scientists" and "Consumer Test Panels." The three promoters of this "mileage miracle" were indicted on eighty-five counts of mail and telegraph fraud by a Federal grand jury in New

York City. . . . The United States attorney handling the case called the promotion a "blatant swindle" and pointed out also that Unitron was bought for 50 cents and sold at $4.95—a substantial markup, indeed, capable of supplying a fast-buck operator with many of the luxuries of life.

The Post Office operates under postal fraud statutes title 18, USC 1341 and title 39, USC 4004 and 4005, and Public Law 86—673. The law requires the Postmaster General to prevent the postal establishment from being used in furtherance of schemes to defraud the public. Postal authorities expend approximately $1.5 million in keeping an eye on and suppressing illegal promotions for lonely heart clubs, offers of employment abroad, business opportunities that promise extraordinary profits for part-time activities, chain letters as well as chain referral selling, "charity" fund raising, classified business directories, and correspondence schools. In a single year over 9000 investigations were conducted by the Postal Inspection Service. Not all of the activities in these fields are completely fraudulent, but many are, and they provide convenient covers for aggressive swindlers. Other frauds include: confidence schemes, failure to furnish merchandise or services for money received, sale of "interests in estates," lotteries, matrimonial schemes, medical frauds, real estate and securities swindles, unordered COD parcels, work-at-home schemes, and a host of other flimflam practices.

THE PRESIDENT'S CONSUMER ADVISER [9]

Two newlyweds, Mr. and Mrs. Leslie Midgley of Hartsdale, New York, rented a car in California recently and were spinning blissfully along the highway when the gas pedal fell off. The rental company was very sorry to learn of this. It was even sorrier when it learned that Mrs. Midgley was Betty Furness of Washington.

Miss Furness has been President Johnson's special assistant on consumer affairs for the last ten months. Being a consumer herself, she is intensely sympathetic to the thousands of other Americans who have written her to complain about goods and services that

[9] From "Betty Furness Wins Over Critics in Her Job," by Nan Robertson, reporter, Washington office. New York *Times.* p 25. F. 23, '68. © 1968 by The New York Times Company. Reprinted by permission.

have deceived them and cost them unnecessary amounts of time and money.

This is not surprising. What is unexpected is that her critics have experienced a complete reversal in opinion about the nation's most famous refrigerator saleswoman. . . . [In March 1967] the tee-heeing was deafening when the President announced that Miss Furness, a former movie actress, radio commentator and television pitchwoman for refrigerators would succeed Esther Peterson, an Assistant Secretary of Labor and a militant lobbyist and crusader. Ralph Nader, the automobile safety critic and industry's gadfly, said at the time that "having her in that position is worse than having no consumer adviser to the President at all." Many others expressed similar views.

Change of Mind

Mr. Nader has since changed his mind. So have members of Congress before whom Miss Furness has testified, as well as her own staff. . . .

Walter Sandbach, the executive director of the powerful Consumers Union, now believes that there is

positively no question that Betty has done a great job in her role as consumer representative. She was one of the major factors, in addition to Ralph Nader, in getting a good meat inspection bill passed last fall—a stronger bill than the Agriculture Department ever thought possible.

It was the first strong meat inspection bill passed in sixty years.

Yet less than a year ago people were laughing as Miss Furness confessed she had rarely done her own grocery shopping and did not know the price of eggs. She hardly needed to: For eleven years as chief television saleswoman for Westinghouse appliances she made $100,000 a year. "Any fool can learn the price of eggs," Miss Furness said . . . , "and I'm going to start learning about the small problems women have today, right away."

Aided by Professionals

Miss Furness started on the job . . . [May 1, 1967] in her suite of eight rooms, six doors down the hall from Vice President Humphrey in the Executive Office Building. Her annual budget was $313,000 and her salary $26,000. Her staff consisted of ten Government "professionals"—four of them borrowed from other agencies, which paid their salaries—plus fourteen clerical workers.

Her key adviser has been Leslie V. Dix, a lawyer long active in consumer affairs and Government, who is her chief congressional expert. "Thank God for Les Dix," Miss Furness said in an interview in her office this week. "He really led me by the hand."

Her first chore was to give a speech before the Credit Union National Association, and Miss Furness was petrified. "I didn't even know what a credit union was," she said. She was equally ignorant on the subject of flammable fabrics, on which she testified before a Senate committee several days after having been sworn in. She was drilled beforehand by Mr. Dix, J. Herbert Holloman, then Assistant Secretary of Commerce for science and technology, and experts on fabrics and fire. "They put me through a hearing. They asked me all of the questions to trap me—and they trapped me," Miss Furness said. She later acquitted herself well before the committee. . . .

[In late 1967] another key person came on Miss Furness's staff: Eleanor Pollock, a newspaperwoman of great skill and experience, to do public relations and speech-writing. "Betty's speeches are not Government speeches," Miss Pollock said. "It's like writing a TV script—completely the spoken word. I don't think you ever find 'input,' 'output' or 'implement' in anything Betty says."

A good example of the forthright way Miss Furness talks, in public and out, is the following excerpt from her testimony on the wholesome meat act . . . November 15 [1967] before a Senate Agriculture subcommittee:

I don't want roaches in my meat, and I don't suppose you do. I don't want to eat meat processed in a filthy plant covered with flies, and I don't suppose you do. I don't want to think about these things while I am eating. And I am sure you don't. Thank you very much.

Mrs. Peterson is considered to have been just as courageous and frank as Miss Furness in the consumer job, and she is more solidly grounded in Government processes. But she suffered under handicaps. When she became the President's consumer adviser in January

1964, there was not the climate for consumer legislation that there is now. Congress has discovered that consumer laws are a fairly cheap way to score points with the voters. Leonor K. Sullivan, Democrat of Missouri, who pushed the truth-in-lending bill through the House said: "The White House just didn't give her [Mrs. Peterson] the cooperation she expected. Once she began attacking business and business began complaining, Esther found she no longer had the President's ear."

Mr. Nader agrees. . . . [He] thinks Betty Furness has the President's confidence and really speaks for the White House. As a case in point, he mentioned her testimony on the meat bill, in which her surprisingly firm public stand on inspection succeeded in overruling Agriculture Secretary Orville L. Freeman. "She used to stand up in front of millions on TV and say: 'You can be sure—if it's Westinghouse,'" Mr. Nader said. "Now she's standing up in front of Congress and saying: 'You can be sure—if it's the White House.'"

EDUCATION FOR CONSUMERS [10]

Betty Furness, President Johnson's Special Assistant for Consumer Affairs, is moving to establish a consumer education program that she hopes will be particularly helpful to residents of poverty areas.

The first step will be the appointment of an education director in her office to develop guidelines for a coordinated attack on consumer ignorance by local governmental and voluntary agencies. . . .

Miss Furness outlined two main objectives. One is to "get information out to consumers on what they are consuming"—on "how to shop, what to look for, how to compare, even how to cook, how to get the most out of what it is you bought." She said the need was especially great in poverty areas "and it's pathetic."

The other chief objective, Miss Furness said, is to improve and expand consumer education in the country's schools. She called this "a really tough nut to crack" because local school officials were

[10] From "Miss Furness Sets Education Drive," by John D. Morris, correspondent with the Washington office. New York *Times.* p 37. D. 4, '67. © 1967 by The New York Times Company. Reprinted by permission.

jealous of their prerogatives and many regarded home economics courses as adequate consumer education.

But even in schools with the best home economics courses, "what are the boys learning?" Miss Furness asked. "I want both boys and girls to learn how to set up a budget, how to buy on time, how to select a used car or furniture, how to rent or buy a home," she said. "Don't tell me these things are being taught today, because by and large they are not."

She called attention to a consumer education program at Lincoln High School in Yonkers, as an exception to the rule. She said the school was achieving "considerable success" in blending instruction in consumer economics into its curriculum. Aside from such exceptions, she said, her office will have the task of "urging, cajoling, preparing materials" to promote the teaching of consumer affairs in schools.

CURRENT PRESIDENTIAL PROPOSALS [11]

President Johnson, in a special message to Congress, proposed . . . [on February 6, 1968] an eight-point program "to protect the consumer—and the honest businessman alike—against fraud and indifference."

Included in the program were suggestions for new powers for the Federal Trade Commission. The main purpose of broadening the commission's authority would be to afford a quickly effective weapon—the court injunction—against home-improvement rackets and other unfair, fraudulent or deceptive practices. . . .

The special message gave some details, and Administration officials added others, of the consumer protection proposals sketched by President Johnson in his State of the Union and Budget Messages.

Points of the Program

In his message . . . the President proposed a program to do the following:

1. Crack down on fraud and deception in sales
2. Launch a major study of automobile insurance

[11] From "President Offers 8-Point Program to Aid Consumers," by John D. Morris, correspondent with the Washington office. New York *Times*. p 1+. F. 7, '68. © 1968 by The New York Times Company. Reprinted by permission.

3. Protect Americans against hazardous radiation from television sets and other electronic equipment

4. Close gaps in our system of poultry inspection

5. Guard the consumer's health against unwholesome fish

6. Move now to prevent death and accidents on our waterways

7. Add new meaning to warranties and guarantees and seek ways to improve repair work and servicing

8. Appoint a Government lawyer to represent the consumer. . . .

The Federal Trade Commission, under legislation proposed in the message today, would be empowered to seek preliminary injunctions against what an Administration spokesman called "any unfair, fraudulent or deceptive practice that needs to be stopped immediately" to prevent "irreparable harm to a consumer." "Too often, and too late," the President declared in his message, "the victim discovers that he has been swindled, that he has paid too much, that he has received inferior work and that he has mortgaged himself into long-term debt. Some even lose their homes."

The proposed law also covers sales rackets "of all types," Mr. Johnson said.

"The FTC," he said, "would be able to obtain Federal court orders to stop fraudulent and deceptive practices immediately while the case is before the commission and the courts."

The commission, under present law, is hampered by cumbersome and time-consuming procedures in moving against most unfair and deceptive trade practices. Issuance of "cease and desist" orders, subject to long court review, is the main procedure now allowed in most cases. Authority to obtain preliminary injunctions is limited by existing law to cases involving fraudulent advertising of food, drugs and cosmetics.

In addition to Federal standards for boats, the President proposed $5 million a year in Federal grants to states that adopt effective regulations covering such things as the education and licensing of boat operators, safety patrols, inspections and testing of boats, and accident investigations.

A Consumer Counsel for the Justice Department

Expanding on an earlier announcement, the President said he would appoint "a consumer counsel at the Justice Department to work directly under the Attorney General and to serve the Special Assistant to the President for Consumer Affairs," Betty Furness. The counsel will "seek better representation for consumer interests before administrative agencies and courts," the President said. "He will be concerned with the widest range of consumer matters—from quality standards to frauds." ...

Attorney General Ramsey Clark said at a news conference that the consumer counsel would not be an assistant attorney general but would have the highest civil service rank—GS18. ... The new officer's main duties would include coordinating consumer protection work now performed by various divisions of the Justice Department. He would also intervene on behalf of consumers in important cases before courts and regulatory agencies, the Attorney General said.

Under the proposed legislation to conduct "intensive studies and set and enforce standards" to control hazardous radiation by television sets, X-ray equipment and other electronic devices, manufacturers would be required to recall defective equipment and devices.

The proposed study of automobile insurance would be undertaken by the Department of Transportation. The President said, "Arbitrary coverage and policy cancellations are the cause of frequent complaint." He also mentioned rising premiums and other various practices as warranting investigation.

Mr. Johnson called for industry's cooperation in providing adequate guarantees, warranties and repairs of automobiles and household appliances. At the same time, he said, the Administration would "determine whether Federal legislation is needed."

The President also recommended completion of congressional action on a number of pending consumer bills he proposed in recent years. These included bills to require full disclosure of interest rates and other finance charges on consumer loans and credit buying, to regulate sales commissions and management fees by mutual invest-

ment funds, to curb fraudulent land sales, and to lessen the hazards
of fires and interstate pipelines.

STATE GOVERNMENTS AND CONSUMERS [12]

The preservation of the integrity of our capital markets and the
protection of the consumer and the businessman who provides the
resources for these markets is the responsibility not only of government and law enforcement but of industry as well.

Industry must share with government the responsibility for cur-
tailing fraudulent and deceptive business practices which affect adversely the consumer and investor as well as the well-being of our
entire economy.

From ancient times until the beginning of the modern era of
electronics and the jet age, the cry of *caveat emptor* in the marketplace was sufficient to warn even the most unwary consumer that
he must give careful attention to the selection of the merchandise
he intended to purchase. There were recognized standards of weight
and measure and most items were simple enough to be examined
so that their quality could be discerned with apparent ease.

With the advent of the gimmick, gadget and electronics age,
vast and varied changes have taken place in the marketplace. There
is little room for the application of *caveat emptor* in the relationship between merchant and consumer. But, a new responsibility,
that of *caveat venditor*, must be added to the code of the marketplace. This means that the seller of goods and services must accept
a new responsibility to assist the consumer.

When I became Attorney General [of the state of New York]
in 1957, I was appalled by the shocking scope of the complaints
received by my office. It was obvious that "false" advertising, "bait"
advertising, fictitious pricing, mislabeling, false claims of under-
selling and related false and deceptive practices were being prac-
ticed with proliferating occurrency. Numerous complaints involving
deceptive business practices were being received by my office, other

[12] From "Consumer Protection by State Legislation," an address by the Attorney
General of New York State, Louis J. Lefkowitz, before the New York State Bar Asso-
ciation, Antitrust Law Section, New York City, on January 26, 1967. Text supplied by
Mr. Lefkowitz. 80 Centre St. New York 10013. '67. Reprinted by permission.

law enforcement agencies and by the Better Business Bureaus, the New York office of the Federal Trade Commission, and the New York City Bureau of Weights and Measures. . . .

Enforcement officials were rewarded with little success when they sought to use the sections of the Penal Law to punish persons engaging in false or deceptive business practices. It must be borne in mind that in criminal cases guilt must be established beyond a reasonable doubt. . . .

I concluded that the criminal statutes and the existing provisions of the General Corporation Law and Executive Law were insufficient to cope with the volume and diversity of unfair competitive practices. I was of the opinion that new legislation authorizing the Attorney General to seek injunctions was needed to deal with the problem.

Accordingly, on my recommendation, Section 396 of the General Business Law was enacted at the 1958 session of the legislature. It empowers my office to seek an injunction against "bait" advertising. Such advertising is defined as advertising published as part of a scheme in which the advertiser intends not to sell the merchandise at the prices stated or not to sell it at all. The bait advertising statute exempts the news media in which the advertising appears.

Action Against Deception

On my recommendation, Section 63 Subdivision 12 of the Executive Law also was amended at the 1959 [New York State] legislative session to include "any person" against whom my office could proceed for an injunction based on "repeated fraudulent or illegal acts" or "persistent" fraud. This very important amendment for the first time authorized proceedings against any person for his individual acts as well as against corporations, in addition to acts involving unincorporated associations. . . .

In 1959, a special committee . . . concluded there was a great need for a clear and comprehensive law prohibiting unfair competition and providing swift and effective remedies for violations. In its view, the best legislative approach to the existing problems was to enact a new statute which would cover those aspects of unfair competition most urgently requiring action.

The special committee recommended a statute which in broad terms prohibited all "deceptive acts or practices." The substantive provisions were modeled after the Federal law. The committee concentrated on false advertising because it felt that this constituted the area in which the gravest derelictions occur. The statute recommended by the committee was introduced at the 1959 session. It condemned false advertising as a deceptive act or practice and empowered the Attorney General and District Attorney to seek an injunction to enjoin such practices.

The path of the proposed legislation was strewn with obstacles at its beginning. While the proposed new measure specifically exempted all news media, and placed full responsibility squarely upon the individual or firm that makes the false claim in an advertisement, strong opposition almost immediately appeared from the New York State Publishers Association as well as the publishers of other newspapers and from radio and television station managers. A cry of "censorship" was echoed back and forth across the State. . . .

Despite the efforts of the special committee . . . and my office, the legislation again failed to pass. It was not until 1963, that a measure, recommended by my office, relating to false advertising was enacted into law. It is Article 22.a. of the General Business Law. There is no provision in the present law, however, empowering the Attorney General's office to obtain an injunction, as the bills which did not pass the legislature had provided.

Under Article 22.a, of the General Business Law, the office of the Attorney General is authorized to bring a civil action against any person, firm, corporation, association or agent or employee thereof, who engages in any of the acts or practices which constitute false advertising. Under this law, false advertising in the conduct of any business or in the furnishing of any service is declared unlawful. The term "false advertising," means advertising, including labeling, which is misleading in a material respect. The statute provides that, in determining whether any advertising is misleading, there shall be taken into account not only representations made by statement, word, design, device, sound or any combination thereof, but also the extent to which the advertising fails to reveal material facts. The law provides a penalty of up to $500 for each violation.

The statute does not apply to newspapers or magazines which carry the advertising, nor to the television or radio station which broadcasts the advertisement. It only applies to the advertiser himself. . . .

Other Areas of Concern

Many other areas where the consumer is at a disadvantage in the marketplace have been the subject of effective legislation enacted on my recommendation.

Following inquiries made by my office disclosing fraudulent and deceptive practices in the sale of television tubes to consumers, the legislature enacted Article 29-B of the General Business Law to make it a misdemeanor and permit my office to seek injunctive relief where it is found that rebuilt, reconditioned or used television and radio tubes are sold as new. The law strikes a blow at the counterfeiting and misbranding of tubes and requires technicians who install second-hand or rebuilt tubes to notify the customer that the tube is not new even though the container of the tube may bear such a disclosure.

Where persistent patterns of fraud are not found, there are, nevertheless, instances where the consumer is the victim of an isolated act or acts which constitute fraud and deception. In many such cases, these acts which might appear to be in violation of a particular statute, even if demonstrated, would not result in a successful proceeding under Section 63 of the Executive Law.

In order to provide an administrative method of settling cases akin to the cease and desist order of the Federal Trade Commission, I recommended to the legislature a measure which was enacted in 1962. It is presently Section 63, Subdivision 15 of the Executive Law, and provides that my office shall have the power to accept an assurance of discontinuance of an unlawful practice, in lieu of instituting an action or proceeding. The authority is limited to those cases where, by statute, the Attorney General already has the power to institute such an action or proceeding.

Another significant feature of this statute is its provision that where evidence is shown of a violation of the assurance of discontinuance it shall constitute prima facie proof of violation of the applicable law in any action or proceeding which thereafter shall be brought.

The sale of used and reconditioned merchandise has become a major part of the economy. When a consumer goes to a "second-hand" store he does so with his eyes wide open and expects that the article he may purchase necessarily has been used.

However, my office uncovered many instances of cases where consumers ... [made] purchases from some retail stores, not generally in the second-hand business, [which] had pushed off on the buyer used, rebuilt, or reconditioned merchandise, as new merchandise. Again, legislation was enacted to help stop this practice. Section 395 of the General Business Law now provides that my office may apply for an injunction to restrain the sale of used merchandise whenever the seller fails to disclose the fact that the merchandise has been used. The law also makes a violation a misdemeanor.

In recent years, increased leisure time and a new demand for recreation and social development probably was responsible for the proliferation of dancing schools, weight control salons, gymnasiums and other establishments which offered a special service to thousands of consumers. Many of these institutions had a high purpose and were operated with due regard for their clients. But many of them did not.

My office, as the result of an investigation, found that some of these individuals and firms were taking an unconscionable advantage of consumers, particularly through high pressure sales tactics which resulted in the consumers signing up for *lifetime* contracts for dancing lessons, weight control treatments, or programs of gymnasium exercise. Some persons were induced to enroll in two and sometimes three "lifetime" courses. Exorbitant fees were charged— for example a sixty-five-year-old woman signed up for two lifetime dancing courses at a cost in excess of $20,000.

Again, with the cooperation of the legislature, a bill which I recommended was passed and is now Section 394 of the General Business Law. It prohibits any of these services from offering lifetime contracts to subscribers. Moreover, it requires that where the payment of more than $500 is involved in an installment agreement, the installment payment cannot exceed the prorated value of actual services by more than 5 per cent and prohibits the assignment of such contracts without the subscribers' written consent.

One of the most recent statutes which has given new protection to consumers became law [in 1966]. It is Section 396, Subdivision 2 of the General Business Law. It prohibits the forwarding or delivery of unordered merchandise to consumers and permits anyone who receives such merchandise to plead as a complete defense in any action brought for payment the fact that such merchandise was not ordered.

This measure will go far to protect consumers who in the past have received such unordered merchandise and have paid for it after being dunned and threatened with embarrassment of a lawsuit to recover the cost.

A very effective weapon which my office has in its fight against consumer frauds is Section 63, Subdivision 12 of the Executive Law. . . . Here . . . there is a clear mandate to the Attorney General to bring an action for injunctive relief "whenever any person is engaged in repeated fraudulent or illegal acts." This section was amended by the legislature on my recommendation to cover "unconscionable contractual provisions." The derivation of the new language added by a 1965 amendment is Section 352 of the General Business Law defining fraudulent acts in the sale of securities, and Section 2-302 of the Uniform Commercial Code which grants to the courts the power to refuse to enforce any contract found to have been "unconscionable at the time it was made."

As the result of an action brought by my office, the Supreme Court in New York County, in a landmark decision which applied this section of the law for the first time, ruled that the practices of a corporation which induced consumers to enter into contracts for the purchase of household appliances, were unconscionable. The court nullified many of the contracts which had been negotiated in such fashion. It is interesting to note that the decision stated that the practices of the company were deliberately fraudulent and maliciously dishonest patterns of doing business with the public.

Procedural Gains

During the 1964 session of the legislature, I recommended a bill which was enacted. It amends the CPLR [Civil Practice Laws and Rules] to clarify language of Section 2302 (A) with respect to the authority of the Attorney General to issue subpoenas without a court order. This authority is a particularly potent weapon to aid my office in requiring representatives of firms and individuals who engage in fraudulent practices to testify and produce books and records. The authority of the Attorney General to issue subpoenas for investigative inquiries is now expressly conferred, whereas previously the power was either in a specific statute or implied from the general language of Section 2302 (2) and its predecessors.

The legislation which has been enacted in the field of consumer protection has been of immeasurable help to my office and other law enforcement agencies in waging a continuing fight against fraud. Without the new statutes, we could not have achieved, in great measure, the success we have. These laws, in some instances, have punitive provisions to penalize the guilty; there are provisions permitting my office to obtain injunctions against the individual or firm which engages in fraud. But aside from substantive provisions, the laws have the value of being salutary deterrents to those who might otherwise embark on a course of fraudulent activity.

The over-all progress we have made in administering and enforcing the consumer protection program in the last ten years has far exceeded our fondest expectations. I say with modesty, New York State has become the leader in the nation in enforcement action and has been the model for other states. Our dedicated and resourceful staff has served more than 100,000 consumers in . . . [1966 and 1967] and in both 1964 and 1965 we have recovered more than a million dollars for aggrieved consumers through adjustment of purchases, refunds on goods and services and in helping the consumer to get full value for his dollar. . . .

The fight against fraud and deception in the sale of consumer goods and service must continue to be pursued vigorously.

A CASE AGAINST GOVERNMENT REGULATION [13]

How can the interests of 200 million American consumers best be served? What are the interests, who are the consumers and who best speaks in their behalf? How much protection and how much freedom of choice in the marketplace should consumers have? What are the values sought by consumers, how much deception is there and by what process do we seek to create a "better informed" consumer? How much conflict of interest truly exists between the business community and the consumer? To what extent should consumer wants and needs be legislated, supervised and controlled by government? As we ponder these questions, without definitive answers, a mushrooming movement of consumer protection is sweeping our country.

This movement finds its expression in many forms. We have commissions studying the performance of our manufacturing and distributive industries and making recommendations for reform. We witness congressional action on a host of regulatory issues such as packaging, labeling, credit, housing and auto safety. The President constantly calls for greater consumer discretion in spending. And we hear increasing talk about the need for organized consumer education and for a new Department of Consumer Affairs. Indeed the entire movement seems destined to destroy the basic tenet on which our government is formed—personal liberty, individual responsibility, and freedom of choice.

As government prescribes values, both social and economic, *for* its people what does it do *to* its people? Is it not time that we give attention to the problems already created by consumer protection legislation which prescribes judgment values for all and limits freedom of choice? Are we indeed to eliminate the right of man to make a mistake?

For Joint Action

This is not another speech extolling free enterprise, as virtuous as it may be. And it is not another speech condemning the efforts of

[13] From "Who Best Speaks for the Consumer?" address delivered at annual meeting of the American Meat Institute, Chicago, September 20, 1966, by Max E. Brunk, professor of marketing, Cornell University. *Vital Speeches of the Day.* 33:247-52. F. 1, '67. Reprinted by permission.

government to create a better environment in which to live. Indeed if there is one thing we do not need it is another hollow contribution to the already outrageous disproportion existing between the supply of and demand for free enterprise speeches. Instead it is my fervent hope that we can cast a little light on the subject of how the business community and government can work together in supplying the wants and needs of man. The history of mankind and the experiences of our contemporary political adversaries in other parts of this small world make it clear that neither can go it alone for each has vital and distinct responsibilities.

When these responsibilities are not clearly defined in the minds of men we find business and government in competition—a competition that eventually can have only one survivor. We must never forget that the constituents of the business community and of government organization are the same but their instruments of support are distinct. Government representatives seek and gain their support at the polling place. The business community seeks and gains its support at the marketplace. A free marketplace is as precious to the welfare of man as a free polling place. There is much confusion on this issue. While it is true that all people are consumers, there is indeed a distinction between the actions of people as consumers and the actions of people in a democratic society. The former are constituents of the business community . . . the latter constituents of the politician.

Procter and Gamble seeks its support by promises of a better detergent . . . the politician by promises of lower taxes or better schools. The ability of either to survive depends on performance. It makes no more sense to restrict the costly advertising efforts of Procter and Gamble within the bounds of propriety than it does to restrict the costly campaign efforts of the politician. In both instances there is opportunity. In both instances there is responsibility. It makes no more sense to legislate truth in packaging than truth in politics, law or matrimony.

To the interests of their own welfare it should be no more difficult for people to understand the importance of a free market than the importance of a free polling place. Unfortunately this is not the case. It is not the case because the business community has done a poor job both of selling and protecting the voting place of its constituents. In the public mind a free market has become increasingly identified as the property of the businessman—a device by which the businessman can freely exploit the consumer by any means at his command.

Much of this misunderstanding stems from the encroachment of government into business. In appealing to consumers—who by definition are nothing more than voters in the marketplace—politicians have found a fertile and promising field. The politician has only to identify some trouble or danger that can be rationalized within restricted value concepts and then announce in the public press what he is doing to correct the situation. Such action results in pitting the interests of society against the business community. This is the consumer movement—a move by which elected government representatives gear their actions to people as consumers rather than as voters—a movement that puts government more and more into the business of providing, first indirectly and then directly, politically prescribed goods and services for consumers. As businessmen and politicians increase their competition is it any wonder that the businessman today finds himself a less welcome guest either in Washington or in our state offices?

Until government becomes directly involved in the production of goods and services, and woe be the day, there is little the politician can do in the way of appealing to consumers with new and better products and services. As a result political actions in the consumer field can only be restrictive in nature. Lacking both productive capacity and the incentive to serve some currently unrealized market opportunity political action in the consumer field is relegated to protectionism. Hence the present movement is appropriately described as a consumer protectionist movement but it should be recognized that this is nothing more than a transitory stage to a government that will ultimately prescribe all consumption values for its people. In such an environment it is no small wonder that we hear an increasing call for consumer education. If people are to be satisfied and vote "right" they must be trained to want that which a benevolent government deems good for them.

The role of government in the marketplace has been that of protecting the public's life and health—of preventing fraud and unscrupulous practices—of stimulating and encouraging competitive private business sensitive to both the changing and unknown wants of our people. And rightly so government should and does protect its people from *unrecoverable* damage. But the emerging philosophy of supervision and control extends far beyond these limits in attempting to protect the consumer from economic injury in purchasing risks. It is my contention that a free marketplace is a far more effective regulator of such risk than legislative action. . . .

Who Is the Spokesman?

This background of concern leads me to my topic. Who best speaks for the consumer? Here we have many choices to debate in terms of the questions raised. Is indeed the spokesman of the consumer to be a Cabinet officer appointed by the President to a newly created Department of Consumer Affairs? Or is the best spokesman the Congress of elected representatives? Does the best spokesman necessarily come from government? Are consumer groups well enough organized and sensitive to consumer interests to be effective spokesmen? How about market researchers or, if education is the key, we certainly should consider the qualifications of the academic community. What role should be played by the manufacturer and the merchant who daily struggles to keep his customers happy?

This indeed is a mammoth task for there is much static in the air. If in our own minds we cannot distinguish between the opportunities and responsibilities of government in serving its voters and the business community in serving its customers how can we hope to resolve the growing conflict between them? Certainly if the politically inspired tide of public mistrust of the business community is to be turned we must start somewhere. . . .

At the present time consumer interests in government are served in a wide variety of ways. A recent congressional study reveals that no less than thirty-three Federal departments are engaged in various phases of consumer protection. This study revealed that these agencies were involved in 118 different consumer protective activities requiring the services of 6,500 full-time employees. In addition there were 178 other programs indirectly related to the consumer interest. . . .

And this is but a small part of the activity that goes on in Washington and at the state and local level where we also have extensive policing of a wide variety of marketing processes extending from weights and measures to sanitation and trade practices. This all adds up to a highy protected consuming public and it raises a number of questions. Would the consumer interest better be served by concentrating these activities in a new Department of Consumer Affairs? Can such a department serve as an effective spokesman for the consumer in the promulgation of new laws and regulations? What interest groups would be most influential with such a department? To what degree should such a department act as intermediary between buyers and sellers?

In the past government has established consumer protection laws and regulations in response to needs as they arise. The administration of these activities has been delegated to agencies and departments accustomed to working with the special businesses involved be it agriculture, finance, commerce, drugs, labor, housing or what not. The proposal for a Department of Consumer Affairs shifts the audience center from supplier to buyer and by this process cuts across our total economy. Because almost every issue of consumer protection is related to the operational idiosyncrasies of the supplier involved, such a department would encounter both conflict and duplication of effort with every other department of government. Certainly it is questionable that such a department could effectively administer without bias all the diverse interests involved.

Implicit in serving as spokesman for consumer needs is the identification and interpretation of consumer values and needs. I submit that it is impossible to identify, classify and catalog the consumer value concepts and needs of 200 million Americans. Any businessman knows this. At very best he as an individual can only hope to serve the wants of a small sector of our population part of the time. I say part of the time simply because the values and needs of any individual consumer also change with each purchasing decision. On top of this, consumer values are both tangible and intangible. If indeed these are truths is it any wonder that we stand at a loss to rationalize the purchasing behavior of our people? Is it any small wonder that we say people sometimes act irrationally? What we really mean is irrational in terms of defined values and being only mortals, at any one time, under any one circumstance we focus on singular material and economic values. My point is simply this. Efforts to reduce the purchasing behavior of man to social common denominators through either education or legislation will serve more to deprive than to enable man to fulfill his wants. It is very important that we distinguish between the proper role of government in protecting its consumers from deceptive practices and the inappropriate role of serving as intermediary between buyers and sellers in making value judgments. A Department of Consumer Affairs geared to an audience of consumers will be concerned more with the latter than the former. With ever expanding regulation of our markets there is perhaps a growing need to protect consumers against governmental actions which restrict the business community from responding fully to the wants of consumers but this is not likely to be forthcoming from a Department of Consumer Affairs.

How effective a spokesman for the consumer the proposed department might be is demonstrated by the past activities of the President's Special Assistant for Consumer Affairs. While it is true that this office does not hold the administrative powers normally entrusted to a cabinet post, it is nevertheless true that much effort has been made to gain consumer, business and labor support for the program during its gestation period. Talks were given, professionally managed press conferences held and consumer meetings scheduled. It should be apparent to the most ardent supporter of the program that consumer interest failed to develop. Participation in the publicly held meetings is indicative of the interest groups from which a new department could be expected to gain its support. They were largely professionals from other government offices, from the colleges and schools, from the press, from labor groups and organizations of various kinds engaged in consumer matters. Characteristically, spokesmen at these meetings seldom spoke as consumers— when they spoke, it was usually in behalf of someone else. Is it not logical that the same representatives will be the influencing force around a Department of Consumers Affairs? At least the evidence strongly suggests that it will not be the consumer.

The Consumer's Role

Apparently the consumer already knows that any remedial action he deems necessary is most directly accomplished as a result of his actions in the marketplace. He also knows that the marketplace respects his actions either when he is in the minority or with the majority. He does not expect to impose his consumption values on his neighbor any more than he expects his neighbor's values to be imposed on him. He clearly sees the so-called proliferation of products in a multitude of package shapes, sizes and design not as deception but as a simple response to his many minority requirements as a consumer. Can you imagine what a canned ham would look like if it were designed to conform to specifications laid down by a democratic consensus of 200 million consumers? To what proportion of the voters would it be acceptable . . . to what proportion deceptive?

In spite of all our efforts to treat them so we must recognize that there is not one universal body of consumers possessing common values. To the contrary the market consists of an endless number of minority groups each seeking special attention. No one law, no one regulation, no one bureau, no one manufacturer, no one retailer can serve them all with equal fairness and satisfaction. Much of the success of a manufacturer or retailer lies in his ability to identify and structure his product to the particular market segment he seeks to serve . . . an action often misinterpreted by those who would apply universal values of consumption to all. Each new protective market regulation reduces the capacity of industry to respond to minority interests. Flexibility to respond to the varied and changing consumer wants is the hallmark of a free market. These are but a few simple reasons a Department of Consumer Affairs can never truly speak for the consumer.

That the Congress serves as spokesman for the voter at the polling place does not mean that it can, or should, serve as spokesman for the consumer in the marketplace. In serving the marketplace, the legislative process at best can only establish general guidelines for all to follow in the prevention of fraud and the maintenance of competition. When these boundaries are violated, Congress finds itself in the hopeless business of determining universal consumer values which transcend the multitude of minority interests previously discussed. Any detailed actions in regulating the marketplace serve to deprive consumer minority groups. This identifies an important distinction between the polling place which rigidly imposes the will of the majority and the marketplace which responds dynamically to all minority interests. . . .

Whenever Congress attempts to regulate the market to serve specific consumer values . . . whenever Congress attempts to speak for the consumer, it ends by delegating the responsibility to some agency of government which it assumes has the omnipotence to do the job. Such contributions to the maze of vague, administratively determined, prohibitive regulations surrounding the marketplace are indeed not the product of one who best speaks for the consumer. . . .

The Role of Academicians

In the light or darkness of the foregoing discussion, we can quickly discharge consideration of the academician as spokesman for the consumer. In his role he neither regulates nor directly serves the consumer with consumptive goods. He merely studies and tries to interpret the complexities of both consumer behavior and the marketplace. Being somewhat removed from the political and business world he deals largely with theory and ideals which he brings to bear through his teachings and writings. The consumer values and interests he stresses are aligned with his special field of interests and this coupled with a lack of authority to protect and responsibility to serve, makes him an inappropriate spokesman for the consumer.

If not the academician perhaps we should consider the so-called consumer organizations we hear so much about these days. If these truly exist they must be secret societies because specific examples are so difficult to identify. Practically all such organizations in final analysis are aligned with some special interest group serving some minority interest seeking to impose their will on all. Few, if any, have widespread consumer support and consequently cannot be taken seriously as spokesmen for the consumer. Indeed the lack of strong and widely supported consumer organizations in this country provides some evidence that consumers now feel adequately protected from damage in the marketplace. One possible exception is the Consumers Union—a nonprofit organization of self-employed persons engaged in testing and recommending consumer products based only on specified physical values of performance. While the value of this service to consumers can scarcely be denied some question remains both as to the adequacy of their testing and the appropriateness of the consumer values appraised.

The recent proposal of Mr. Donald Turner that the Consumers Union be subsidized with Federal funds, to permit more adequate testing and dissemination of findings, is both enlightening and alarming. Apparently this Assistant Attorney General who is in charge of the Antitrust Division feels that a more adequate job of testing consumer products needs to be done and that consumers can be given a set of value standards under government direction and sponsored propaganda by which to judge purchases. Indeed it is not surprising that Mr. Turner seeks out someone with the omnipotence to determine consumer values for he, more than anyone else in government, has been given a comparable assignment by a Congress that can neither define competition nor specify how they expect Mr. Turner to maintain it.

The Role of Business

Lastly in our search we turn to the business community—to the manufacturers and retailers who are directly involved in supplying goods and services to the consumer. Not only does the manufacturer and retailer have the benefit of the advice and council of government officials, politicians, academicians, consumer groups and their own market research and experience but also they get the first and most forceful reading on consumer response in the marketplace. Unlike the politician who goes to the polls every few years to get a performance reading the marketer gets his reading each day.

Surely now we have identified who best speaks for the consumer. But if this be true why do the manufacturer and marketer make so many mistakes? Why do you sit here trying to figure out what it is that the consumer wants? Why do you produce so many goods and services that won't sell? Why do you spend so much of the "consumer's money" trying to convince her in every conceivable way to buy your product or shop at your store?

I believe that the answer is simple. There is no true spokesman for the consumer other than the actions of the consumer herself. Try as she might she will rationalize her actions but she cannot explain them in full. That is why she cannot tell you what new or modified goods and services would better serve her needs. In marketing research I have spent the better part of my life ringing consumer doorbells in a futile effort to get them to tell me how some product or market service can be improved or what new products or services they want only to find that in response they failed either to visualize their alternatives or identify the true values to which they in final analysis respond. The consumer, in her mute but effective way, can only bring all her value considerations to bear in response to what is offered her. She has her own built-in protective device. If you displease her . . . if you do not offer her the best alternative . . . if indeed you deceive her in terms of her own values, she simply and quickly votes "no" in the marketplace. That is the miracle of the free market. Those who argue that the consumer acts irrationally or is continually deceived in the marketplace simply fail to identify or accept the true values which the consumer deems important. It takes far more than economic rationality to explain consumer behavior.

In serving the consumer interest the real question is not who best speaks for but rather who best answers the consumer. The reply can only be the manufacturer and distributor . . . those who actually serve her consumption needs . . . those who have given this nation the highest standard of living the world has ever known.

The great tragedy of our time is that the consumer does not fully appreciate this. She does not realize that the business community serves her needs in spite of, not because of, public market regulation. More and more she seems willing to go along with government protection in the marketplace. She fails to realize that this protection carries with it an implicit cost in her economic, emotional and physical well-being. Why is the consumer unaware of the true role of the business community?

Fundamentally this results from the political invasion of the marketplace by government . . . from political appeal, shifted from people as voters at the polling place to consumers as voters at the marketplace. Nothing better illustrates the technique than the current rash of red herring investigations of food marketing margins and corporate profits. This diversionary tactic of fingering a scapegoat for the high prices that result from government overspending is both deceptive and politically dishonest. This fraud on the American public pits the consumer against the business community and establishes a base for an ever increasing political interference with the marketplace.

In trying to understand consumer response to political appeals we must recognize fundamental changes in the thought processes of our people. With each passing year we become more a nation of employees and less a nation of individual entrepreneurs having inherent appreciation of business ethics, aims and purposes. Again, with each passing year, we tend to forget that our population becomes younger, more educated, more wealthy, more independent in its thinking . . . that in such an environment ideologies take on greater importance and meaning. Could it be that the business community has become so absorbed in competing for consumer patronage that it has neglected these emerging ideologies and left a void into which the politician has moved? At least the public today seems to anticipate and expect business opposition to any and all matters of consumer protection . . . opportunities preempted by the politician. How can the business community close this void? How can it more effectively compete with the politician in gaining a positive image of interest with the consumer? Surely the business community has far more capacity than the politician to deliver in the fulfillment of her ideologies. . . .

Clearly and dramatically you must demonstrate how the meat industry, within the law, acts to protect the consumer interest. You must show how the protection you provide is the cheapest and most effective form of protection. You must show how current antitrust regulations make it both expensive and difficult for your industry members to work together in setting standards for consumer health and safety and in self-disciplining marketing practices. You must use more of your advertising skills to show how the meat industry acts to protect and serve consumers. To reach the right audience this may mean that you will have to upgrade your copy to the mentality of a mature adult.

Each one of you have the responsibility of finding a better, more refreshing way of telling the story of how both profits and marketing margins in the meat industry are used in serving the consumer interest. As if to apologize you talk about the small profits you make. Have you ever thought of talking about how those profits are plowed back into developing a better, more satisfying product?

And while we are talking about the numbers game why don't you do something either to correct or expose to public view the misleading and false statistics on average meat prices collected by the Bureau of Labor Statistics? Similar problems exist with many other publicly used measures of market performance such as your and the farmer's share of the consumer's food dollar, which create false public impressions.

Certainly meat industry members should conspicuously demonstrate their responsibility in serving the public welfare by overt acts of direct competition with government programs of consumer protection and education. At the same time industry executives must devote more of their time to direct government service.

And, in conclusion, as you sit around the conference table in your many trade association activities, you have the capacity to identify many other problems in your relationship with government which should be converted into positive opportunities.

A CASE FOR MORE GOVERNMENT PROTECTION [14]

The rhetoric of consumer protection in recent years has been as impressive as the reality of the consumer interest expendability. The

[14] From "Ralph Nader Faces the Nation's Business," address by Ralph Nader to the National Consumer Assembly, Washington, D.C., November 1967. Co-Op Contact (publication of the United Housing Foundation). p CC 4-5+. Winter '67. Reprinted by permission. Mr. Nader is the author of Unsafe at Any Speed and a leading advocate of consumer interests.

thunderous acclaim for such legislation or pending legislation as the truth-in-lending bill, the cigarette-labeling law, the truth-in-packaging bill is not measured commensurately by the forcefulness of the legislation in fact. I sometimes think that industry is perfectly willing to trade off a particular name with a particular legislation, such as truth-in-lending, in return for very effectively gutting its adequate provisions. The threat is very often not so much whether we have consumer-protection legislation but whether or not we have a law or a no-law law—a no-law law which simply deludes the consumer, deludes the public into thinking it receives a protection when in fact it is the industry which receives the protection by a bizarre, ironic twist.

The cigarette-labeling act is a perfect case study here. This act effectively excluded any action for five years by the states and cigarette-protection legislation. It effectively excluded the Federal Trade Commission from any action. It effectively excluded any attendance to the problem of advertising in cigarettes. And it effectively provided a convenient defense in civil liability suits to the cigarette industry by requiring a warning on the package that it may be hazardous to health. This was a bill which the tobacco industry simply could not do without. And yet it was touted as a consumer-protection legislation.

I think that it is important to recognize that, even when laws are passed that are adequately drafted, the administration of these laws can effectively render them impotent. A good example here, in terms of abundant authority and not so abundant administration and enforcement, affects the Federal Trade Commission, which I think can be called the Government's better business bureau with all that implies.

A Myth Perpetuated

One of the sad by-products of the Federal Trade Commission's pronouncements and activities, with some outstanding exceptions, is that the Commission has perpetuated a myth over the years that deceiving the consumer or harming the consumer is primarily a fly-by-night phenomenon in terms of the fringe participants of American business that really isn't the mainstream of solid, upstanding businessmen—it is those near-bankrupt firms that are besmirching the reputation of American business in general.

I find this rather difficult to appreciate in the light of the facts. I don't think the packaging problem in this country just affects a few fringe marketeers. I don't think the credit practices in this country just affect a few corner pawn shops. I don't believe that the electric price-fixing conspiracy which bilks the consumers to the tune of hundreds of millions of dollars over the three decades of the conspiracy, ending in 1961, simply was a result of a few fly-by-night electric firms. I don't think the lack of safety in automobiles is due to a few small garages who hand-make some hazardous automobiles. I don't think the adverse effects of drugs and lack of adequate disclosure is due to makeshift pharmaceutical houses in the back of a large pharmacy or two. I think in effect that the problem of consumer protection is very much the problem of American business in general, very much the problem of the largest industry and the largest company, very much the problem of those who should be able to perform far better and far more responsibly than those fringe businesses who might be up against the wall in terms of their sheer economic survival.

A recent example is the Greyhound Bus Company, which has been routinely using, until very recently, balled regrooved tires, regrooving them again and again, leading to accidents in which people were killed and injured—leading to accidents whose investigations remain secret within our Department of Transportation, because the motor carrier industry wrote that secrecy into legislation years ago—the kind of practices by Greyhound which have never received enforcement. . . . The first enforcement process is now underway in New Jersey for a Greyhound accident involving regrooved tires. The maximum penalty on conviction is $500.

Now, are we dealing with a company—a small bus company—whose back is against the wall, and for sheer survival is trying to cut costs on tires? No. We are dealing with the largest bus company in the world—a bus company whose liquid capital is so embarrassingly ample that it owns outright 27 Boeing 707/727 planes, which it leases to the airlines.

Inadequate Fulfillment

I think another problem of the Federal Trade Commission as an example of the inadequate fulfillment of its authority comes in areas where there is absolutely no doubt, where there are absolutely no shades of judgment possible in terms of the course of action that should be pursued. For years the odometers have been overregistered —that is, they have been designed in a way to make you feel as if you are traveling more than you are. Now there is a far more than a mere psychological consequence to this rigging of a basic measurement device. When an odometer is rigged to the plus side, you tend in the aggregate to trade in your car faster. You think your car is a little older. Your warranty runs out in terms of mileage. You tend to pay more to a rent-car-company who, of course, collects on the mile. You also tend to think you are getting better gas mileage, which is something the auto companies want desperately to convey to their buying public. And yet this problem of odometer deception, which has been going on for years with the knowledge of the Federal Trade Commission, did not achieve attention until about 1964 when the National Bureau of Standards decided to rewrite the standard. Now, even though the standard was rewritten, odometers are still capable of being overregistered and still capable of meeting the new standard. But the important point in the history of the odometer is the statement finally conveyed by an old hand at the Federal Trade Commission, who when confronted with the suggestion that it was the National Bureau of Standards who took the initiative, not the Federal Trade Commission, blurted out, "That is utter nonsense. Why, we have been concerned with odometer problems since the Hoover Administration."

Meat Inspection

Another problem dealing with laws, their adequacy in drafting and their administration and the responsibility of a consumer protection agency or department in government deals with the recent meat inspection controversy. Here we have the Department of Agri-Business, misnamed the Department of Agriculture, which for years has had the responsibility—Upton Sinclair wrote the book, *The*

Jungle—for roughly sixty-one years to inspect meat packaging, meat processing, slaughter houses, the trade in interstate commerce. Unfortunately, over the years, there has been a substantial traffic in intrastate meat shipment, and at present 25 per cent of all processed meat in this country does not cross state boundaries and therefore escapes the Federal inspection service. This is eight billion pounds a year.

The surveys of the Department of Agriculture in 1962 on a state-by-state basis revealed what everybody in the industry knew all along, but revealed it authoritatively, that there were three basic and endemic problems affecting the intrastate meat industry. The first was a kind of Gresham's law: believe it or not, bad meat is good business. And bad meat drives out good meat in some of these local markets. Bad meat, meaning the 4-D animals: trafficking in dead, dying, diseased or disabled animals, where, for example, the cancerous portions of the cow are simply cut out and the rest of the carcass sent to market.

The second problem: unsanitary, grossly unsanitary, conditions in the meat-processing plant. The reports here are so nauseating, and they are not made by laymen, they are made by veterinarians or inspectors—the reports here are so nauseating on a state-by-state basis that nobody could ever read them through at one sitting and remain with his equanimity. These descriptions reveal, for example, the prevalence of roaches, flies and rodents having free play of the meat-processing plant and willingly or unwillingly finding their way off into the meat vats, the paint flakings from the ceilings dripping and dropping onto exposed food. There was some indication that some of these inspectors couldn't get close to the plants because of the overwhelming potency of the odor, and sometimes they did get close enough, but they couldn't talk clearly with the manager because of the flies that screened out his visibility.

The third problem deals with what do you do to make this product—this 4-D product—presentable to the consumer. Of course, here the wonders ingenious of modern chemistry come into play. A seasoning agent, preservatives and coloring agents do the job, and the basic natural detection processes of the consumers are masked.

He is no longer able to taste, smell or see diseased or contaminated meat. And he pays out his money accordingly. This problem was documented in 1962, and our friendly Department of Agriculture felt it was more important to protect the meat-packing industry than to protect the consumer. So for five years they have sat on these reports—for five years they did nothing until there were hearings at the congressional level and new reports were forthcoming to confirm the 1962 report.

With all of these problems, with all of these disclosures, the House of Representatives by a vote of 140 to 98 passed a weak and meaningless meat inspection act, as far as the control of intrastate plants is concerned. The alternative bill, called the Smith-Foley Amendment, would have brought roughly 98.5 per cent of all the meat processing in the country under Federal inspection. That bill was defeated.

Lobby Seeks Money

The interesting aspect of the situation is the immediate disclosure after the passage of the legislation that a large meat-packing trade association had recommended in a letter to its members . . . that they contribute contributions to the political campaigns of friendly congressmen (mind you, at the same time, these congressmen were considering the meat inspection bill and its alternative); the recommendation was that the contributions be from $25 to $99 —$99 so that the individual contributors need not be disclosed. Now this situation was brought to the attention of the chairman of the House Agriculture Committee, who favored the weak bill. He immediately replied to the director of this trade association that it was a terrible thing to have done—it placed the meat industry in a potentially untenable situation, that it jeopardized the meat bill which the meat industry favored. In other words, all his concern was directed towards the welfare of the meat industry and being able to escape Federal inspection of its intrastate activity.

Not a word in these letters, mind you, as to the welfare of the consumer. Not a word to the need to publicize this impropriety the moment it was located. In effect, the entire effort of some of these friendly congressmen at the House Agriculture Committee was to sweep it under the rug, to squash it, to keep it from being disclosed so that nobody learned exactly what is going on.

I think it's time to look into this situation with a far greater degree of thoroughness. A congressman who is not known to make very flippant and unsubstantiated remarks has said that he has never seen a bill where so much money was involved in the negotiation. I would think a congressional investigation particularly in the context of the campaign-financing reform that is now pending in Congress would be well advised.

There are other aspects of the meat bill which I think give us good lessons to ponder. These are the kinds of lessons, incidentally, which are similar to the battles over . . . water pollution, soil contamination, chemical and radiation hazards, inadequately tested and prescribed drugs and so forth. At first, it is a misnomer to think that the meat problem is one of tiny, filthy meat-packing plants. Swift and Armour are involved here—they have plants which operate exclusively within state boundaries. Surveys of these plants have shown very substandard conditions and it's quite clear that Swift and Armour as well as their smaller colleagues have been engaging in marketing of meat which has no place in being sold to the American consumer.

Not Only Lip Service

The role of the Administration is interesting here as well. At the last hour the Administration finally neutralized the Department of Agriculture, with no small achievement, and came out basically through its consumer office and Miss Furness with a stronger version of legislation. [The stronger bill was enacted in December 1967.— Ed.] That is very encouraging, but obviously that is only the first step in the position which I think the Administration should reflect. The Administration should not only be on the record for consumer protection; it should be on the ramparts. It should not only give lip service. It should give muscle service. It often intrigues me why the Administration is so successful and so powerfully lobbying for the supersonic transport, that great sensational mass alarm clock that is on the horizon, and be so ineffective, so reticent and so inhibited when it is asked or expected to lobby for meat inspection laws and for auto safety appropriations to give just two recent examples. I think it is encouraging that next year will be the first year that the Federal Government will spend more money on traffic safety than the safety of migratory birds. But I don't think it says much for our allocation of our resources in this land. Not when we can spend some $45 million next year for a problem that is killing 53,000 Americans and injuring over 4.5 million at the same time that a nuclear submarine is costing $110 million. That's just one nuclear submarine.

I think, in other words, that it is time not just to give a serious look at the Administration policy on consumer protection but to what extent it is going to really begin to effectively advocate it beyond rhetoric and to effectively reallocate some of our resources to this area. The legislation doesn't mean much if you don't have money to administer it with. I think, for example, it is a reflection of a distorted sense of values when we can spend last year $150 million on highway beautification and about $10 million on highway safety. The presumption here against that kind of allocation of resources is that the best way to get more money for traffic safety is to see that the blood gets on the daisies....

It is necessary to stop concentrating exclusively on the syndromes of the consumer protection phenomena, and penetrate through to the more basic preconditions which give rise to the syndrome. I think, to be more specific, that one side of the coin may be consumer protection but the other side of the coin is, inescapably, corporate reform. I think it's important to go to the roots of the problem so we don't place ourselves in the situation of running around trying to plug the holes in the dike before it overflows. And in this sense, in the sense of the controllability of catching these problems before they arise, the focus on corporate reform is a must. For example, corporations now should be required to meet much stiffer disclosure requirements. They should be required to tell specifically the safety performance of their products so that the marketplace can be put to work in a way which they will not perhaps fail.

I think that it is an important distinction to make, that however much lip service corporations give to the free market, they are really more interested in the control market. If they were interested in the free market they would tell you the safety performance of their products, such as automobiles, so that the consumer can go to the marketplace and compare make and model and make his choice on the basis of quality and in this way generate the feedback mechanism of the marketplace by rewarding good workmanship and penalizing shoddy workmanship. This is the kind of disclosure requirement that really puts the market to work to a higher degree of efficiency.

Penalties Needed

Another requirement, I think, is to beef up our sanction for corporate violation. We are reaching a point in this country where it is no longer possible to sweep under the rug the tremendously wide double standard operating between the penalties imposed on individual behavior and the penalties imposed on corporate behavior. Corporate behavior, more and more, is being immunized from legal accountability. You see the decline in criminal penalties in safety legislation for knowing and willful violation. And look at the disparity. A driver negligently driving down the highway kills an individual. He can be subjected to manslaughter charges and put in jail for negligence. But a manufacturer can willfully and knowingly leave a defective product on the marketplace in such a way that it can take human life, under the new auto safety legislation, and there is no criminal penalty whatsoever. Only civil penalties—the kinds of penalties that don't penetrate the corporate framework . . . [exist.] A perfect and recent example here is the Lake Central Airlines crash in March [1966] with thirty-eight people killed in a crash directly attributed to a soft piston problem with the propeller coming off and ripping into the fuselage. It so happens that Allison, the division of General Motors that builds the engine and propeller, had known about this defect some time before the crash, and instead of advising all operators to immediately ground this plane and disassemble it, which is the only conclusion that could be reached once a defect of that seriousness is located—instead of doing this, they sent a vague advisory saying why don't you have an oil check to see if the oil's contaminated by metal filing. And the doomed plane was given an oil check and the result was negative. And thirty-eight people died because the Allison Division was worried about its corporate image and was worried about facing up to this problem. The fine by the Federal Aviation Agency was $8,000—about $200 a head. Perhaps one must not be too harsh with the FAA, they resisted General Motors pressure to reduce the fine to $4,000.

Research a Necessity

Another area deals with research and development, which is no longer a luxury on the part of the large corporations, it is an absolute necessity, because simple inaction can bestow on the public welfare and safety immense cruelty. Simple inaction [in] researching ways to clean up the internal combustion engine, or find an alternative, has resulted in a critical air pollution problem in our cities, inaction stemming back many, many years by industry leaders. And so, the problem of research and development, the problem of requiring them to shoulder a responsible portion of this innovative input is one that is on the first agenda, in my judgment.

Standards Most Important

And a final area deals with standards, and I think this is probably the most important one; that when safety bills are passed, when standards are set for products, that these standards be set by government, that they not be set by private standards groups, who have succeeded in insinuating into legislation their particular standards and codes. That is, government must make these standards, allowing democratic access to the administrative process on the part of both industry and public groups. This is an extremely critical problem. It is one which will be more critical the next year, as the United States Standards Institute of America begins its campaign to receive a congressional charter, take on the aura of a quasi-governmental agency and in effect begin to determine the level of standards of safety in product after product. . . .

Antitrust a Key Issue

[Now, I want to make one comment on competition.] Competition is not out of date, but it is still a very viable principle; however unviably it is enforced. The problem with competition and instilling a competitive flavor, even in the more concentrated industry, is that antitrust enforcement has not been what it should be. And in fact a recent commentator such as Professor Galbraith has begun to erect a theory of the American economy based on the failure of antitrust. Instead of saying antitrust hasn't failed per se, its enforcement . . . [has] failed. They are taking the failure as a fact of life—as an enduring fact of life—and building a new theory of oligopoly and concentration.

I think recently the disclosures that, indeed, the antitrust division has done work on the possibilities of applying the Sherman Act to General Motors will have very salutary effects—I think one of these effects we all should try to further is that antitrust should no longer be the province, the exclusive province of a few Justice Department lawyers and a few house counsels for large companies, that antitrust is intimately related to consumer protection, that antitrust should be a discussion throughout America and that the limitations of antitrust should be known as well as the potential of antitrust and the possibility of extending the grasp of the mechanism for competition by additional legislation. I think that it is an eminently reasonable public issue to debate whether or not General Motors should be broken up. I think the concentration of power represented by a company that grosses $2.3 million an hour twenty-four hours a day, more than any other foreign government except Great Britain and the Soviet Union, that the concentration of economic and political power here is one which may clearly transcend the tolerance of a democratic society. The ability of General Motors to in effect delay, thwart and block efforts in California, and now running near the second decade of completion to develop cleaner internal combustion engines is an impressive example of how even against the second largest and now the largest state of the union, against the unity displayed by California, they have succeeded again and again in delaying until about two years ago. One of the reasons of course is the concentration of power here. Another reason is that there is no penalty for delay. There is no penalty for inaction. So I think looking at antitrust and concentrated industry there should be an important program for any consumer body to consider. It is not, for example, trivial that a Grand Jury in Los Angeles for the last year has been hearing evidence presented by the Justice Department on its allegation that the auto industry has combined in restraint of trade to restrain the development and marketing of auto exhaust control devices. You see, antitrust relates to the air we breathe, to the safety of the product we buy, to the quality, to its price. It not only deals with economic efficiency or the lack thereof—it deals with the insecurity of life and limb.

Protection Required

I think a stake here in the whole consumer movement is not just the quality of the goods, not just honest pricing, which of course improves our allocation of resources, but also in my judgment the most critical area of all—an area which might be termed as the area of bodily rights. The right of one's physiological integrity from being invaded, assaulted or destroyed by the harmful by-products of industrial products and processing.

Now against this threat we have something to be encouraged by. Unlike prior errors in history we now have a technological period where we can actually program innovation in human welfare and safety. We can invent the technological future if we will to do so. And no better was this stated than by the vice president of Ford Motor Company, Donald Frey, who said of his industry that basically our engineers can do anything we want them to do; they "can invent practically on demand." Now with an increased capability like this the ethical imperatives to act become all the more insistent; because I think it is fair to say that to a substantial degree that what we should do proceeds from what we can do. And as the capability increases . . . so does our ethical requirement to follow through.

It is a serious disservice to consumerism, if I may use a recent term coined in a deprecatory manner by one of our large business executives last year. It is disservice to consumerism to view this as a threat to the private enterprise economy or to big business. It is just the opposite. . . . Of course, the upshot of consumer protection, when it succeeds, is simply to hold industry to higher standards of excellence, and I can't see why they should object to that kind of incentive. And hopefully, as it gains momentum, the consumer movement will begin to narrow the gap between the performance of American industry and commerce and its bright promise.

III. BUSINESS AND CONSUMER PROTECTION

EDITOR'S INTRODUCTION

Traditionally business attitudes toward consumer interests have been summed up in the slogan "Let the buyer beware." Today the scales are shifting and consumer and government attitudes can be summed up in the slogan "Let the vendor beware." But however strong consumer power has been, the real struggle over regulation and standards for production and marketing has taken place between government and business. A long business-government dialogue has prevailed in America, especially since the late nineteenth century antitrust legislation.

This dialogue has often been at cross purposes and indeed still is. It is this dialogue which is explored in this section. Two economists writing in the *Harvard Business Review* examine the nature, assumptions, and conflicts of the dialogue. Their penetrating analysis helps to explain the conflicting views expressed by government and business representatives in the other articles in this section.

In the second selection Victor H. Nyborg, president of the Association of Better Business Bureaus International, explains the work performed in the consumer's interest by the Better Business Bureaus.

Next, Miss Betty Furness of Westinghouse TV fame, now Special Assistant to the President for Consumer Affairs, speaking to a marketing audience, urges businessmen to be leery of a growing trend in favor of protectionism in foreign trade and relates that problem to those of the consuming public. The section closes with statements by a Federal representative and a businessman, in which the dialogue continues on general economic conditions affecting manufacture and marketing, the role of advertising and its regulation, and the very practical problems which manufacturing plants must cope with in meeting certain government regulations.

THE DIALOGUE BETWEEN
BUSINESS AND GOVERNMENT [1]

In recent years government and business spokesmen alike have advocated a "dialogue" between their two groups for the reduction of friction and the advancement of the general good. Yet, all too often, this is a dialogue that never happens. Rather, what passes for dialogue in *form* is often a sequence of monologues *in fact,* wherein each spokesman merely grants "equal time" to the other and pretends to listen while preparing his own next set of comments. Obviously, this is not always the case; and, if taken literally, it tends to minimize some real progress being made.

Our aim here is to try to facilitate and stimulate that progress by exploring what lies behind the dialogue that never happens and by suggesting what can be done—on both sides—to develop more meaningful and effective business-government interactions.

In this context, we link "government spokesmen" with "critics." Naturally, not all in government are critics of business, and vice versa. However, almost all critics seek redress of their grievances via government action and seek government spokesmen to present their views "in behalf of the public."

Our primary focus will be in the field of marketing—particularly selling and advertising—which is perhaps the most controversial and most frequently criticized single zone of business. Marketing seems to be the area where achieving true dialogue is most difficult and where business and government spokesmen most seem to talk past each other.

Before examining why this takes place, let us look at two comments on advertising that illustrate the lack of dialogue. The first comment is that of Donald F. Turner, Assistant Attorney General in charge of the Antitrust Division of the Justice Department:

There are three steps to informed choice: (1) the consumer must know the product exists; (2) the consumer must know how the product performs;

[1] From "The Dialogue That Never Happens," by Raymond A. Bauer, professor of business administration specializing in consumer behavior, and Stephen A. Greyser, assistant professor, both at Harvard University Graduate School of Business Administration. *Harvard Business Review.* 45:2-4+. N.-D. '67. © 1967 by the President and Fellows of Harvard College; all rights reserved. The authors are co-authors of *Advertising in America: The Consumer View.*

and (3) he must know how it performs compared to other products. If advertising only performs step one and appeals on other than a performance basis, informed choice cannot be made.

The other comment is that of Charles L. Gould, Publisher, the San Francisco *Examiner:*

No government agency, no do-gooders in private life can possibly have as much interest in pleasing the consuming public as do . . . successful companies. For, in our economy, their lives literally depend on keeping their customers happy.

Double Entendres

Why do business and government spokesmen talk past each other in discussing ostensibly the same marketplace? We think it is because each has a basically different model of the consumer world in which marketing operates. This misunderstanding grows from different perceptions about a number of key words.

The first word is *competition.* The critics of business think of competition tacitly as strictly price differentiation. Modern businessmen, however, as marketing experts frequently point out, think of competition primarily in terms of product differentiation, sometimes via physical product developments and sometimes via promotional themes. The important thing is that price competition plays a relatively minor role in today's marketplace.

Some of the perplexity between these two views of competition has to do with confusion over a second word, *product.* In the critic's view, a product is the notion of some entity which has a primary identifiable function only. For example, an automobile is a device for transporting bodies, animate or inanimate; it ordinarily has four wheels and a driver, and is powered by gasoline. There are variants on this formula (three-wheeled automobiles) which are legitimate, provided the variants serve the same function. Intuitively the businessman knows there is something wrong with this notion of the product because the product's secondary function may be his major means of providing differentiation (an auto's looks, horsepower, and so on).

Then there is the term *consumer needs,* which the business critic sees as corresponding to a product's primary function—for example, needs for transportation, nutrition, recreation (presumably for health purposes), and other things. The businessman, on the other hand, sees needs as virtually *any* consumer lever he can use to differentiate his product.

Next, there is the notion of *rationality*. The critic, with a fixed notion of "needs" and "product," sees any decision that results in an efficient matching of product to needs as rational. The businessman, taking no set position on what a person's needs should be, contends that any decision the customer makes to serve his own perceived self-interest is rational.

The last addition to our pro tem vocabulary is *information*. The critic fits information neatly into his view that a rational decision is one which matches product function and consumer needs, rather circularly defined as the individual's requirement for the function the product serves. Any information that serves that need is "good" information. To the businessman, information is basically any data or argument that will (truthfully) put forth the attractiveness of a product in the context of the consumer's own buying criteria.

Exhibit I summarizes our views of these two different models of the consumer world. We realize that we may have presented a

Exhibit I: Two Different Models of the Consumer World

Key words	Critic's view	Businessman's view
Competition	Price competition.	Product differentiation.
Product	Primary function only.	Differentiation through secondary function.
Consumer needs	Correspond point-for-point to primary functions.	Any customer desire on which the product can be differentiated.
Rationality	Efficient matching of product to customer needs.	Any customer decision that serves the customer's own perceived self-interest.
Information	Any data that facilitate the fit of a product's proper function with the customer's needs.	Any data that will (truthfully) put forth the attractiveness of the product in the eyes of the customer.

somewhat exaggerated dichotomy. But we think the models are best demonstrated by this delineation of the pure views of contrasting positions, recognizing that both sides modify them to some extent.

Views of Human Nature

A review of our "vocabulary with a double meaning" and the two models of the consumer world shows that the critic's view is based on a conviction that he knows what "should be." In contrast, the businessman's view is based on militant agnosticism with regard to "good" or "bad" value judgments which might be made (by anyone) about individual marketplace transactions.

The businessman's view of human nature may be the more flattering, perhaps excessively so. Certainly, the marketer's notion of "consumer sovereignty" compliments the consumer in attributing to him the capacity to decide what he needs and to make his choice competently even under exceedingly complex circumstances. It also sometimes challenges him to do so. This perhaps undeserved flattery glosses over some obvious flaws in the market mechanism. It is rooted in the belief that this mechanism, even though imperfect in specific instances, is better than administrative procedures for regulating the market.

The critic takes a far less optimistic view of human nature— both the consumer's and the seller's. He thinks that the seller often (sometimes intentionally) confuses consumers with a welter of one-sided argumentation. Such information, in the critic's eye, not only lacks impartiality, but usually focuses on secondary product functions and is not geared to consumer needs.

Both sets of assumptions are, we think, at least partially justified. Customers do have limited information and limited capacity to process it. This is the way of the world. Furthermore, there is no reason to believe that every seller has every customer's interest as his own primary concern in every transaction, even though in the long run it probably is in the seller's own best interest to serve every customer well.

All of this disagreement comes to focus on a point where both business and government are in agreement; namely, modern products are sufficiently complex that the individual consumer is in a rather poor position to judge their merits quickly and easily. The businessman says that the customer should be, and often is, guided in his judgment by knowledge of brand reputation and manufacturer integrity, both of which are enhanced by advertising. The critic argues that the customer should be, but too seldom is, aided by impartial information sources primarily evaluating product attributes.

These conflicting views of vocabulary and human nature are reflected in several specific topic areas.

Brands and Rating Services

One of these areas is the relationship of national branding to consumer rating services, the latter being a traditional source of "impartial information" for consumers. Somehow the crux of this relationship seems to have escaped most people's attention: consumer rating services are possible *only because of* the existence of a limited number of brands for a given product. In order for a rating to be meaningful, two conditions are necessary:

1. *Identifiability*—the consumer must be able to recognize the products and brands rated.

2. *Uniformity*—manufacturers must habitually produce products of sufficiently uniform quality that consumer and rating service alike can learn enough from a sample of the product to say or think something meaningful about another sample of the same product which may be bought in some other part of the country at some later time. This is a seldom-realized aspect of national branding.

It is generally assumed by both groups that the "consumer movement" is basically opposed to heavily advertised branded goods. The stereotype of *Consumer Reports* is that it regularly aims at shunting trade away from national brands to Sears, to Montgomery Ward, or to minor brands. Yet the one study made of this issue showed that, contrary to the stereotype, *Consumer Reports* had consistently given higher ratings to the heavily advertised national brands than to their competitors.

Ideological Blindness

What we have here is an instance of the consumer movement and brand-name manufacturers being ideologically blinded by different models of the market world. The consumer movement concentrates on the notion of a product having a definable primary function that should take precedence over virtually all other attributes of the product. True, some concessions have recently been made to esthetics. But, on the whole, the consumer movement is suspicious of the marketing world that strives to sell products on the basis of secondary attributes which the consumer movement itself regards with a jaundiced eye.

The evidence available to the consumer movement is that, in general, national advertising is *not* accompanied by poorer performance on primary criteria. But the consumer movement fails to realize that it *takes for granted* the central claim for advertised branded products—namely, that by being identifiable and uniform in quality, they offer the customer an opportunity to make his choice on the basis of his confidence in a particular manufacturer.

But the manufacturers of nationally branded products and their spokesmen have been equally blind. First of all, we know of none who has pointed out the extent to which any form of consumer rating must be based on the identifiability and uniformity of branded products. The only situation where this does not apply is when the rating service can instruct the consumer in how to evaluate the product—for example, looking for marbleizing in beef. However, this is limited to products of such a nature that the customer can, with but little help, evaluate them for himself; it cannot apply to products for which he has to rely on the technical services of an independent evaluator or on the reputation of the manufacturer.

Moreover, except for such big-ticket items as automobiles, consumer rating services usually test products only once in several years. In other words, they rate not only a *sample* of a manufacturer's products, but also a sample of his performance *over time*. Thus, if one "follows the ratings" and buys an air conditioner or a toaster this year, he may buy it on the rating of a product made one, two, or three years ago. Similarly, if one buys a new automobile, he depends in part on the repair record (reported by at least one rating service) for previous models of that brand.

In large part, then, consumer rating services are devices for rating *manufacturers!* This is not to say they do not rate specific products. Sometimes they even draw fine distinctions between different models from the same company. But in the course of rating products, they also rate manufacturers. What more could the manufacturer ask for? Is this not what he claims he strives for?

Basic Dichotomy

More to the point, what is it that has kept the consumer movement and brand-name manufacturers from paying attention to this area of shared overlapping interests? Neither will quarrel with the exposure either of factual deception or of product weaknesses on dimensions that both agree are essential to the product. This is not where the problem is. The problem is that the manufacturer *sells* one thing and the rating service *rates* another.

The concept of a "product" that dominates the thinking of rating services and the thought processes of those who suggest more "impartial evaluation information" for consumers (e.g., Donald Turner of the Department of Justice and Congressman Benjamin Rosenthal of New York) is that a product is an entity with a single, primary, specifiable function—or, in the case of some products such as food, perhaps a limited number of functions, e.g., being nutritious, tasty, and visually appealing. The specific goal of many proposed ratings—with their emphasis on the physical and technical characteristics of products—is to free the customer from the influence of many needs to which the marketer addresses himself, most particularly the desire for ego-enhancement, social acceptance, and status.

The marketer, oddly enough, tends to accept a little of the critic's view of what a product is. Marketing texts, too, speak of primary and secondary functions of a product as though it were self-evident that the esthetic ego-gratifying, and status-enhancing aspects of the product were hung on as an afterthought. If this is true, why are Grecian vases preserved to be admired for their beauty?

And why did nations of yore pass sumptuary laws to prevent people from wearing clothes inappropriate to their status?

We shall shortly explore what may lie behind this confusion about the nature of products. First, however, let us examine another topical area in which similar confusion exists.

"Materialist Society"

The selling function in business is regularly evaluated by social commentators in relationship to the circumstance that ours is a "materialist society." We could say we do not understand what people are talking about when they refer to a materialist society, beyond the fact that our society does possess a lot of material goods. But, in point of fact, we think *they* do not understand what they are talking about. Let us elucidate.

At first hearing, one might conclude that criticism of a materialist society is a criticism of the extent to which people spend their resources of time, energy, and wealth on the acquisition of material things. One of the notions that gets expressed is that people should be more interested in pursuing nonmaterial goals.

The perplexing matter is, however, that the criticism becomes strongest on the circumstance that people *do* pursue nonmaterial goals—such as ego enhancement, psychic security, social status, and so on—but use material goods as a means of achieving them. Perhaps the distinctive feature of our society is the extent to which *material* goods are used to attain *nonmaterial* goals.

Now there are many ways in which societies satisfy such needs. For example, there are ways of attaining status that do not involve material goods of any substance. Most societies grant status to warriors and other heroes, to wise men who have served the society, and so on. Often the external manifestation of this status is rigidly prescribed and involves signs whose material worth is insignificant: a hero wears a medal, a ribbon in his lapel, or a certain type of headdress, or he may be addressed by an honorific title.

However, in societies that value economic performance, it is not uncommon for material goods to be used as status symbols. Indians of the Southwest, for example, favor sheep as a symbol even to the extent of overtaxing the grazing lands and lowering the economic status of the tribe. As a practical matter, this might be more damaging to the welfare of the Navaho than is the damage that many low-income Negroes do to their own individual welfares when, as research shows, they insist on serving a premium-priced brand of Scotch.

Many of the things about which there is complaint are not self-evidently bad. Art collecting is generally considered a "good thing." But take the worst instance of a person who neurotically seeks self-assurance by buying art objects. Clinically, one might argue that he would do himself a lot more long-run good with psychotherapy even though, when one considers the resale value of the art objects, he may have taken the more economical course of action. Similarly, it is not self-evident that the promotion of toiletries to the youth as a symbol of transition to manhood is inherently cruel—unless the commercials are especially bad! It is clear, however, that there is no societal consensus that the transition to manhood should be symbolized by the use of toiletries.

What seems to be the nub of the criticism of our society as a materialist one is that simultaneously a great number of non-material goals are served by material goods, and there is no consensus that this should be so. Behind this is our old friend (or enemy): the concept of a product as serving solely a primary function. In the perspective of history and of other societies, this is a rather peculiar notion. Who in a primitive society would contend that a canoe paddle should not be carved artistically, or that a chief should not have a more elaborate paddle than a commoner?

Much of the confusion over the words on our list seems to be a residue of the early age of mass production. The production engineer, faced with the task of devising ways to turn out standardized products at low cost, had to ask himself, "What are the irreducible elements of this product?" This was probably best epitomized in Henry Ford's concept of the automobile, and his comment that people could have any color they wanted so long as it was black. Clearly, Ford thought it was immoral even to nourish the thought that a product ought to look good, let alone that it should serve various psychic and social functions.

But all this was closely related to the mass producer's effort to find the irreducible essence of what he manufactured. This effort broke up the natural organic integrity of products, which, at almost all times in all societies, have served multiple functions.

Many writers have called attention to the fact that in recent times our society has passed from the period of simpleminded mass production to that of product differentiation on attributes beyond the irreducible primary function. As yet, however, we do not think there is adequate appreciation of the impact of the residue of the early period of mass production on thinking about what a product is. In that period even very complex products were converted into commodities. Since each performed essentially the same primary function, the chief means of competition was pricing.

Products as Commodities

At this point, we shall argue that the thinking of those who criticize the selling function is based on a model for the marketing of commodities. This factor does not exhaust the criticisms, but we believe it is at the core of present misunderstandings over the concepts on which we have focused our discussion.

On the one hand, to the extent that products are commodities, it is possible to specify the function or functions which all products in that category should serve. It follows that a person who buys and uses such a commodity for some purpose other than for what it was intended has indeed done something odd, although perhaps useful to him (for example, baseball catchers who use foam-rubber "falsies" to pad their mitts). In any event, it is possible both to specify the basis on which the commodity should be evaluated and the information a person is entitled to have in order to judge that product. A person searching for a commodity ought first to find out whether it serves this function and then to ask its price.

On the other hand, to the extent that products are *not* commodities, it is impossible to expect that price competition will necessarily be the main basis of competition. Likewise, it is impossible to specify what information is needed or what constitutes rational behavior. Is it rational for a person to buy toothpaste because its advertiser claims it has "sex appeal"? Presumably people would rather look at clean than dingy teeth, and presumably people also like to have sex appeal—at least up to the point where it gets to be a hazard or a nuisance.

But it does not follow, insofar as we can see, that ratings—or grade labeling—should discourage product differentiation or the promotion of products on a noncommodity basis. If the consumer were assured that all products in a given rating category performed their primary functions about equally well, could it not be argued that those attributes which differentiate the products on other functions would then become increasingly interesting and important? Or, to be more specific, what makes it possible for "instant-on" TV tuning to be promoted—other than a presumed agreement, by both manufacturer and consumers, that the TV set performs its primary function little better or worse than its competition?

This is a facet of competition not appreciated by the opponents of grade labeling, who have argued that it would reduce competition. Perhaps it would be more helpful if the opponents of grade labeling first gathered some evidence on what has actually happened to competition in countries where grade labeling has been introduced. (The head of one major relevant trade association recently told one of us that he knew of no such research.)

Toward More Information

Readers will note that we have indulged in considerable speculation in this article. But most of the issues on which we have speculated are researchable. Relatively little, for example, is really known about how businesses actually see themselves carrying out "the practice of competition," or even about the actual competitive mechanisms of setting prices. Furthermore, in all of this, there is no mention of the *consumer's* view of these various concepts or of his model of the marketing process. To be sure, we can be reasonably certain of some things. For example, we know that consumers do regard products as serving needs beyond the bare essentials. Yet it would be helpful to know far more about their views of the over-all marketing process.

What we propose as a worthwhile endeavor is an independent assessment of the consumer's view of the marketing process, focusing on information needs from his point of view. Thus, rather than businessmen lamenting the critics' proposals for product-rating systems and the critics bemoaning what seem to be obvious abuses of marketing tools, both sides ought to move toward proposing an information system for the consumer that takes into account *his* needs and *his* information-handling capacities while still adhering to the realities of the marketing process. . . .

This proposal is but an extension of the conclusions reached by members of the American Marketing Association's Task Force on "Basic Problems in Marketing" for the improvement of relations between marketing and government. In brief, along with suggested studies on the influence of government policies and programs on corporate marketing decisions, a special study was recommended in the area of consumer-buyer decision making and behavior: "It is of the highest importance to investigate the impacts of the host of governmental regulations, facilities, aids, and interventions upon the quality and efficiency of consumer-buyer decision making." The report went on to state that, particularly in light of the generally recognized drift from *caveat emptor* toward *caveat venditor*, "abundant basic research opportunities and needs exist" in the area of government impact and consumer-buyer behavior.

Certainly there is a crying need for more information and, as we have tried to illustrate, for fresh analytic thinking on almost all of the issues on which government and business are butting heads.

THE ROLE OF BETTER BUSINESS BUREAUS [2]

To the business community, the cry for "consumer protection" means the mounting efforts of public figures and their political and philosophical allies to mobilize the immense, potent masses who are supposed to cherish above all else their ability to buy. This pre-

[2] From "Business Ethics and Consumer Protection," by Victor H. Nyborg, president of the Association of Better Business Bureaus International. Reprinted from *Freedom of Information in the Market Place*, papers and summaries of discussion sessions of the ninth annual Freedom of Information Conference December 4-6, 1966, at the Freedom of Information Center, School of Journalism, University of Missouri, Columbia. Ovid Bell Press, Inc. Fulton, Mo. Copyright 1967 by the Freedom of Information Center. p 49-56. Reprinted by permission.

occupation with "concern for the consumer" has become almost all-consuming; it is generating and accelerating at a time when the American economy is flourishing as never before. Today, goods and services are available in greater variety and abundance than heretofore experienced in human history, and at minimal prices. The entire process is a marvel to the world.

Paradoxically, no longer do the critics of our enterprise system withhold their attacks until the system is faltering, as in the years of the Great Depression. Now they criticize and attack when times are at their very best. While these assaults are united enough to suggest that they are master-minded, the response has thus far been sporadic and fragmented. On this one point there can surely be agreement: in this century there has been no continuing, connected, centrally directed or coordinated, intelligent action in support not of business per se, but of business as related to the national interest.

The key, I believe, is found in the words "national interest." In the present charged atmosphere, many in Washington and elsewhere have come to think of the words "consumer interest" and "national interest" as synonymous. But are they, really? Is it in the national interest to project consumers as a separate, identifiable body?

Is it in the national interest to attempt to set up consumers as a class, to implant in the public mind that government alone is interested and able to protect the public welfare? To set one segment of society against another, to sow seeds of suspicion and distrust, can only lead to a breaking down of the traditional marketplace relationship between sellers and buyers and, if allowed to persist, could cause economic as well as political consequences. It is the relationship between buyers and sellers that must be nurtured and protected in the national interest.

It seems to me that the answer lies in somehow introducing into the national consciousness some recognition of the weight that should be given not to consumers, not to business, not to farmers or labor or to any other segment of society, but to the "national interest."

What is needed is a *voice*, one that can embrace all elements of society and, by providing a proper forum, seek out the national interest as it affects business, consumers and the government. It must be a forum that is acceptable because it is patently and demonstrably honest, and therefore already has an acceptance; a forum that can speak not just to professors, and in tomes, but also on the receptive wave-length of the majority; a forum with effective and convincing influence.

I believe, as many others do, that the Better Business Bureaus, a half-century-old, nationwide organization created by business and faithfully supported by business over the years, can provide that forum.

The history of the Bureaus and of their past role in national life shows a good record of service in some 139 communities and market areas across the land. While the Bureaus are supported by business, they enjoy the approval and patronage of a wide mass that goes under the general description of consumers. They are regarded as fair, diligent and useful; the citizen's friend in the marketplace.

The Better Business Bureaus have been chartered "to build and conserve public confidence in advertising and in business generally." This has been their prime objective and function since 1912.

The need for self-policing, confidence-maintaining activity by business has persisted and grown over the years. It is evidenced by the spread of local Bureaus across the country and by the ever-increasing volume of consumer, business, civic and government resorts to the Bureaus for services covering the whole business-consumer spectrum.

In the past half-century, particularly since World War II, the Bureaus have become a closely integrated network, with 126 offices in the continental United States. Some 2,500 businessmen, representing all segments of marketing in all lines of enterprise, serve as bureau officers and directors, determining policy, financing and administrative direction. They also serve on BBB committees concerned with voluntary trade practice work.

Each local Bureau is comprised of all business firms which support it. They vary in size and operation according to the size of the community or market area and membership. Each is a nonprofit corporation. The membership elects annually the board of directors, whose officers in turn name the local Bureau executive who employs a professional staff of full-time employees ranging in number from about forty-five for a metropolis such as New York or Los Angeles to three in Salt Lake City.

We consider 1946 to be a "breakthrough" year. At that time there were 69 local Bureaus supported by 32,000 business firms, providing a dollar support of $1.2 million. In 1966 there were 139 units supported by some 100,000 business firms, of all sizes and in all lines of enterprise, with a dollar total of close to $7 million.

All of these Bureaus are organized into the Association of Better Business Bureaus International. The fourteen Bureaus in Canada and other countries are an integral part of the network. The international organization services the local Bureaus, including the New York based National Better Business Bureau, and it also reflects, nationally and internationally, the extensive experience and information gathered through the entire network. The Association, I should add, is financed through dues paid by member Bureaus and currently operates on an annual budget of just under $200,000 with a full-time staff of eleven.

It can be seen that the Better Business Bureau complex is or has been essentially a grass roots organization wherein its great strength and influence has been felt. However, the influence of these community or market-area Bureaus is much greater than their size and number might indicate, for they work with the business community, with law enforcement agencies, with print and broadcast media, with civic organizations and educational groups. Each Bureau reaches out in many ways to collectively bring great influence to bear on the national scene.

The Bureaus receive inquiries and complaints and gather facts relating to business-customer relationships; when necessary, following investigation, offenders are asked to adjust marketplace practices, on a voluntary basis. Where this procedure is not successful, the pertinent information is referred to the appropriate authorities. It is worth noting that something less than 2 per cent of about

50,000 advertising cases investigated each year have to be turned over to the authorities as a last resort.

Nationally, these activities constitute a treasure-house of business-consumer information. We receive nearly 3.5 million contacts from consumers annually (in contrast, contacts with the public in 1946 were barely 1 million). Of these requests for information and assistance, nearly 90 per cent are inquiries concerning the reliability of companies with whom consumers are interested in doing business.

This is an almost complete reversal of percentages. Twenty years ago, the complaints outnumbered the inquiries. This suggests not only the growing effectiveness of the Bureaus; it indicates the ever-widening influence of the Bureaus and the confidence the consuming public places in them. . . .

At the national level, requests for information and assistance or complaints involving national advertising and selling are referred to the National Better Business Bureau. It operates, as do the local Bureaus, in consulting with and providing a myriad of guides, aids and reports to national business firms and to national advertising media. This national Bureau is separately financed by some 2,000 companies and associations which provide approximately a half million dollars annually.

It can be said, then, that the Better Business Bureaus have a continuous, intimate and pervasive involvement in business-consumer relationships, all of it as a result of the desire of American business to keep its own house in order, to build and maintain a strong marketplace relationship with customers on whom it depends for profits, for its very life, today and in the future. . . .

According to *Sales Management,* our population is approximately 195 million. City populations served by the Bureaus in the United States total about 117 million, or about 62 per cent. When we include the National Better Business Bureau, with its 900 smaller-community Chamber of Commerce members which participate in the Bureau's "Community Protection Program," we estimate that the population served directly and indirectly by this combined network is well above 80 per cent of the national total.

To serve such a large percentage of the population requires the cooperation of public media. . . . It seems obvious that the Better Business Bureaus could not perform effectively were it not for the cooperation of the nation's print and broadcast media. Neither would the consuming public receive such a high measure of protection without the BBB information which the media freely carry.

While the Better Business Bureaus are business-supported, this does not mean that they are strict protagonists for business as such. While they also serve the public (consumers all) they are not consumer organizations in the accepted sense. Although they cooperate closely with government offices and agencies in matters relating to the regulation of advertising and selling practices and consumer protection, they are not the handmaidens of government.

This is demonstrated not only in the 3.5 million contacts made by the public; it can be seen in the approximately ten thousand requests received last year from a wide variety of organizations, including labor unions and consumer groups. In addition, the Bureaus handled nearly six thousand requests for information and assistance from various government agencies and offices—national, state and local.

Of greatest importance, in today's scheme of things, the Better Business Bureaus are regarded by consumers as friendly, interested participants in consumer affairs, as organizations eager to help and determined that all shall be fairly served.

In short, the Better Business Bureaus have become widely known and are regarded favorably by the public, and by most government authorities, as *public interest* rather than *special interest* organizations. Business has made the Bureaus what they are: agencies of business in the national interest. By serving the needs of the consuming public, they serve the business community.

While the present Better Business Bureau network has been productive and of value, the current political, economic and social changes necessitate restructuring of the Bureaus and vast expansion of their facilities and services if they are adequately to meet the challenge of the times. While consumerists of one variety or another are accelerating programs which, intentionally or otherwise, discredit all of American business, sowing seeds of suspicion and discontent, business needs to devise new ways to demonstrate again to the public, convincingly and dramatically, the dependability of American business and the mutuality of the business-consumer interest. . . .

Steps are under way now to restructure, upgrade and expand the Better Business Bureaus' facilities and services. In brief, this new effort aims to:

1. Broaden the dialogue between buyer and seller in such a manner that the consumer may continuingly and increasingly voice his opinion of business practices, or his complaint of misrepresentation or unfair treatment, to the producer and retailer through the Better Business Bureaus

2. Institute a broad, massive program to publicize the work of the Better Business Bureaus in order that *all* consumers may know that they have in their own communities a source to which they may turn for information and assistance in their individual problems with business

3. Increasingly encourage and assist business to correct, voluntarily, practices which have been or may become the subject of justified public complaint at both the local and national levels

4. Speak out with authority, nationally as well as locally, on matters involving advertising and selling practices affecting both business and consumers, whether such matters are in the area of local, state or Federal regulation.

5. Conduct a stronger nationwide, comprehensive and continuing program of public education, through the dissemination of facts for intelligent buying—primarily through mass media, but also in cooperation with schools, community groups, government and the interested business community

Several substantial steps already have been taken. For one, we have activated the Better Business Bureaus' Research and Education Foundation, organized in 1952, which has an "absolute charter" from the Board of Regents of the New York State Department of Education. This Foundation will be the vehicle by and through which broad industry support—financial, moral and active—will be sought. The Trustees of the Foundation (ten have accepted invitations to serve and others will be invited as we progress) include national figures in commerce, industry, communications, banking and consumer affairs. We hope to add leaders in education and other fields of endeavor and thus bring to the Better Business Bureau complex the highest caliber of responsible leadership.

It also is our desire to bring to the councils of government the experience of Better Business Bureaus at the grass roots. We want to establish a liaison and relationship built on mutual understanding and confidence and respect for each other's areas of interest and capabilities not only in protecting the public from chicanery and fraud, but as a reflection of what responsible business is doing to regulate itself in the public interest. We can offer a unique, trusted communications channel. We can offer an expertise on consumer affairs of benefit to all concerned.

To this end we have opened a Washington Office for National Affairs. Its activities, initially, will be limited, but we shall expand as needed and as funds are received from business to support this and other activities.

At the community level, Bureaus in nearly thirty cities have established or are planning to establish Better Business Bureau Consumer Affairs Councils, composed of leaders of business, education, government, labor, religion and of course consumers. It is hoped that these councils will provide the forum to bring into focus problems affecting consumers and their relationships with business. They will offer an opportunity for carrying out a continuing dialogue, to find possible solutions to present and future problems, and will recommend courses of voluntary action in the best interests of all concerned.

As a further step we plan to conduct regionally, and eventually nationally, symposiums and seminars relating to specific problems affecting consumers. Such meetings of leaders in various fields should produce a constructive body of information which can guide business and government and education in developing constructive courses of action affecting the national interest.

In another area we are recommending that the Bureaus set up systems and procedures whereby periodic checks and special studies can be made on national trends relating to advertising and selling practices, and actions taken on them. This activity will provide an additional body of knowledge, useful to the Better Business Bureaus themselves in originating or redirecting programs tailored to meet the needs uncovered. This activity, too, will be helpful to those concerned with public policy and consumer protection, and with maintaining a healthy atmosphere in the marketplace.

THE CONSUMER'S ADVOCATE SPEAKS TO RETAILERS [3]

In the increasingly depersonalized American marketplace, the retail merchant is generally the only man the consumer can get his hands on. He knows exactly where you are and he can be fairly sure you'll be there tomorrow. The producer, the packager, the shipper and the marketer are not quite so accessible. They can slip neatly behind the merchant's skirts and never be seen again, if the consumer is irate enough. And, so, many of the responsibilities of the entire new marketplace fall mercilessly upon your shoulders. For the most part, I think you have handled those responsibilities well. . . .

But you must know, gentlemen, that a new day is coming for the American marketplace. The consumer has found his voice and started to use it. The supermarkets have felt the effect of the newly-articulate consumer, so has the auto industry and so, most assuredly, has the meat-packing business. . . .

This voice is going to sound in other directions now and while I would not suggest that there is a department store in the country as irresponsible as one of the bad meat houses, I do think there is a great deal more that the retail merchant—and especially this association—can do to serve the consumer.

Now, I don't expect to convince you to abandon your opposition to inclusion of revolving credit in the truth-in-lending bill; although I must say I can't understand one of your chief spoken objections to those provisions. I can't understand why so many merchants say it is too difficult to explain the full interest charges on revolving

[3] From remarks by Betty Furness, special assistant to the President for consumer affairs, before the National Retail Merchants Association, New York City, January 9, 1968. Mimeographed text supplied by Miss Furness. The White House Office. Washington, D.C. 20500. '68.

credit. One and a half per cent per month certainly adds up to 18 per cent for twelve months. . . .

But there are other things that retail merchants could do in the way of consumer service and net themselves a host of satisfied customers in the bargain.

What the consumer needs and the merchant can readily provide is, in a word, *information*. . . .

Today's marketplace is vast and bewildering. It stretches across the nation and in fact, across the earth. We have products from everywhere, vast numbers of products, complicated products, products we don't need, products we do. They're all out there on the shelf together and while the United States is notably committed to freedom of choice, it is also concerned about providing people with the means to make a choice.

Here is an opportunity for the merchant and, I think, a responsibility. You can help greatly with educating the consumer toward products and how to use them, toward good buying habits and budgeting. You can start programs of your own, you can use the media, you can encourage and aid the schools, civic groups and public agencies in establishing continuing consumer education for youths and adults and especially the poor among us. You can use your influence as astute buyers to prod manufacturers and marketers about simpler instructions and better labeling. The NRMA's [National Retail Merchants Association] guide for improved and permanent care labeling of consumer textile products is a very good example of this and I am waiting with great interest to see how closely manufacturers follow this voluntary guide. . . .

There is another urgent area that deserves your attention both as retailers and consumers. As you know . . . a large batch of new trade bills . . . [has been introduced in Congress.] These were protectionist bills which would have established restrictive quotas on a mammoth number of products imported into this country every year, no few of them products of great interest to your businesses—glass and chinaware, silks and sewing machines, shavers, watches, typewriters and textiles, footgear, linens, sporting goods, costume jewelry, raincoats, radios, and a long list of others.

Most of this legislation was removed from consideration . . . but if anyone here is under the impression protectionism is a dead issue, I want you to know that . . . these bills will [again] be before both Houses. . . .

I do not need to tell you what the effects on the economy will be if these bills are passed; nor do I need to remind you that the first to suffer will be retail business. You are having a great time these days with imports. You know how many stores have whole floors and festivals and special promotions devoted to them. I think it is clear the American consumer wants imported goods and is willing to pay for them.

But more importantly, we must remember the history of protective trade legislation in this century, what it can do to our economy and the world trade upon which that economy so completely depends. The Smoot-Hawley Act [1931], you will recall, was one of the most disastrous pieces of legislation ever aimed at our economy. Within four years after enactment of Smoot-Hawley, the total dollar value of world trade had dropped by two thirds. When the United States decided not to import, other countries naturally did the same and our own exports fell by 70 per cent. I don't think we can afford a repeat of protectionism. If we try hard enough, we can protect our economy right out of existence. We must be sure that these protectionist bills are defeated.

If the bills should be passed, about $3.5 billion worth of imports would never reach the United States. Several countries have already implied to the State Department that there will be retaliation and, of course, we could expect nothing else. . . . We might just as well not have bothered with the Kennedy Round [of tariff cuts] nor enacted the Trade Expansion Act of 1962. . . .

I have been urging the consumer and I urge you today to let the Congress know how you feel about this legislation, that the country does not want it enacted. . . .

You will recall that the Trade Expansion Act contained provisions which were designed to help industries, individual businesses and workers who might be injured by increased imports resulting from our new tariff concessions. These original provisions have not worked out as well as was hoped when the law was passed in 1962.

The act, as many of you know, provides for Federal aid to injured businesses and industries in the form of technical assistance, low-cost loans, loan guarantees and tax relief. It also provides Federal assistance for workers hurt by increased imports by offering them retraining or relocation aid.

That's fine. The trouble comes when someone starts applying for the assistance. In order to be eligible, it must be proved that tariff concessions were *the* major cause of increased imports and that these increased imports were *the* major cause of injury to the firm or whoever the applicant is. In no case have businesses or workers been able to prove both points because in our immensely complicated economy too many factors are involved to prove what is *the* major cause of economic shifts. The Administration intends to ask the Congress . . . to liberalize these provisions.

To keep the lanes of trade open we must be prepared to help those who may be adversely affected by imports. If we want expanded trade then we have a responsibility to provide speedy and substantial help for any worker, or firm or industry that has suffered from this increasing trade.

Retail business has a great interest in world trade, not only because you are selling a ballooning number of imports, but because your businesses, like all businesses, depend upon a sound economy. We will need your help to insure the continued stability of the American marketplace.

ADVERTISING AND COMPETITION [4]

Although there are many aspects of advertising that deserve critical study, I should like to discuss briefly today the question of whether advertising and similar promotional effort is likely to enhance the growth of monopoly in our economy. As we all know, the protection and promotion of a competitive economy is one of our basic governmental policies, and one which we believe to be em-

[4] From an address by Donald F. Turner, Assistant Attorney General in charge of the Antitrust Division of the United States Department of Justice, prepared for delivery before the Briefing Conference on Federal Controls of Advertising and Promotion sponsored by the Federal Bar Association and the Foundation of the Federal Bar Association in cooperation with the Bureau of National Affairs, Inc., June 2, 1966, Washington, D.C. Mimeographed text supplied by Mr. Turner. United States Department of Justice. Washington, D.C. 20530. '66.

inently sound. It is therefore quite appropriate to ask whether advertising hinders in any significant way the achievement of competitive goals; and, if it does hinder in one or more respects, what public corrective policies might be appropriate.

Let me begin with an obvious point. Advertising provides economic benefits to society, benefits which lie chiefly in providing highly useful information. . . .

Nevertheless, while advertising provides gains to society in the form of expanded information about firms and products, we need to consider, also, the nature of the costs which exist and how these are likely to balance with potential gains. All economic activities involve some cost in that they are associated with the using up of resources. This applies as much to the production of advertising messages as to the production of automobiles. Whether in some industries advertising costs are excessive in relation to what we get out of them is an important and difficult question. But my primary concern today is the relation of advertising to competition and monopoly power. . . .

There is no doubt that advertising efforts comprise an important form of rivalry among firms. Whether what appears on the TV commercial is a pretty girl, soft music, or demonstration, the advertiser's message usually is that one product is better than another. At the same time on another channel, or on the same channel at another time, someone else is likely to be inviting listeners to "move up" to a competing product. This is competition of a kind. We should recognize, however, that this form of rivalry is likely to be considerably different in economic effect from those forms of competition which are concerned with the prices established in the market, and the possibility at least exists that the former may be at the expense of the latter.

Advertising outlays affect not only the rivalry which exists among established firms, but also they are likely to have an important influence on conditions affecting the entry of new firms into the marketplace. While consumers may not accept the view that one product is better than another simply because a pretty girl or a famous person says so, they at least are introduced to the names of specific firms and products, and this tends to distinguish established products from those produced by small firms and new ones. What has become important is not so much the context of an advertising message, but rather the mere fact that it has been advertised. Thus, we note the frequent description of a product as "advertised in *Life*." When a consumer . . . decides to buy an established brand rather than a cheaper but unknown product, he may simply be doing his best to cope with the problem of uncertainty and to minimize the risks to him that the product will not do the job for which he is buying it. Because of this quite expectable behavior, a new entrant typically is likely to be compelled to sell at a price below that of established brands or else incur heavy selling costs in penetrating the market. This helps to explain the phenomenon of unbranded products which sell at prices substantially below those of heavily advertised products, even where there is little real difference between them.

To an extent, the increased barrier to entry created by advertising is a price we have to pay for providing consumers with information. But when heavy advertising and other promotional expenditures create durable preferences going beyond the relative superiority of the product, resistant to anything but major countervailing promotional campaigns, we may well question whether the price has not become too high. . . .

Traditional antitrust policy has repeatedly stressed the relationship between the conditions of entry and the existence of monopoly results. It is specifically on this basis that a number of business practices have been attacked as imposing unacceptable restraints on competition. We should hardly be unconcerned if heavy advertising outlays lead both to more concentrated market structures and to the establishment of high monopolistic prices, and it seems clear that they can and do.

A recent study of consumer goods industries found a significant correlation between the proportion of industry sales devoted to advertising and the average profit rates which were earned. Industries with high advertising outlays tended to earn profit rates which were about 50 per cent higher than those which did not undertake a significant effort. Since, moreover, average profit rates in this study reached nearly 8 per cent after taxes on stockholders' equity, it is likely that these additional gains represent monopoly rewards. They represent price levels which can be explained only on the basis of restrictions on competition. . . .

Advertising and Concentration

Heavy advertising expenditures may promote industrial concentration in a number of ways. In a competitive industry we normally expect to find firms entering and leaving the market during any given period of time. Although the exit of firms will continue, entry will be made more difficult as a result of the barriers created through extensive advertising. To the extent that consumers are unable to evaluate the relative merits of competing products, the established products may have a considerable advantage and it is this advantage that advertising messages tend to accentuate. High entry barriers interfere with the normal process through which increases in demand are met at least in part by new firms.

A further significant factor is the existence of economies of scale in advertising and other forms of promotion. To the extent that larger firms can provide more messages per dollar than their smaller rivals, they will have a strong competitive advantage, and this will be so even if smaller firms spend proportionately as much. Economies of this sort lead directly to the expansion of larger firms relative to their smaller rivals and thereby to more concentrated market structures. These advantages, moreover, may be held not only by firms which have a large share of specific markets, but also by those who deal on a nationwide basis in a number of related product areas.

It is in this respect that the quantity discounts given by television networks raise serious questions. While these discounts may in part represent real cost savings, I believe it highly doubtful that the savings should be passed along to purchasers of television time. If the discounts have the effect of accentuating the growth of larger firms and of promoting a tendency toward concentrated market structures throughout consumer goods industries, it may well be appropriate public policy to prohibit or at least drastically limit them, even if this means higher network profit margins for large purchasers than for small. . . .

What are the most appropriate methods of dealing with such problems? There is some room for dealing with the adverse consequences of heavy advertising and other promotional expenditures within the confines of antitrust law. . . . If it should be deemed appropriate to permit mergers of a particular kind to be defended on the ground that they promote substantial economies of scale, the defense should not extend to promotional economies.

I would also suggest that it would be quite appropriate to impose, for a period of time, an absolute or percentage limitaton on promotional expenditures by a firm or firms that have obtained undue market power through violations of the Sherman Act. A classic purpose of a remedial decree in such cases is to dissipate the consequences of unlawful acts, and if limitations on promotional expenditures would help, they are appropriate even though the promotional expenditures as such were and are lawful.

There may be other corrective measures which can be developed under antitrust law, but as of now I believe the most effective remedies are along other lines. One avenue is an expansion of the law on false and misleading advertising. While this may make some contribution, however, regulation of this sort involves terribly difficult problems. . . .

The Need for Information

I believe the most promising approach is to introduce new sources of consumer information. It is the extent of uncertainty about the relative merits of competing products which contributes to the large effect of advertising, and this suggests that Government policies be directed toward neutral vehicles of information which tend to deal directly with the uncertainty. We all know that such consumer research organizations as Consumer Reports tend to promote informed consumer judgment, and we can reasonably surmise that reports of that kind, if generally circulated, would significantly limit the ability of advertising to enhance degrees of monopoly power, to say nothing of enabling consumers to spend their dollars more fruitfully. A similar service exists for physicians in the form of the *Medical Letter*, which is published by a group of physicians, and designed to supply technical information about the therapeutic value of new drugs. In both of these areas, a major difficulty is that these publications are produced by nonprofit organizations and that they frequently face difficulties in obtaining the funds required for adequate testing and evaluation. One prospective solution would be governmental efforts in this direction, either direct Government evaluation and publication, or financial support for private organizations of this type. In the case of drugs, for example, there is much to be said for providing Government funds to the organization which publishes the *Medical Letter* so that its publications may be supplied free to all doctors. In addition, the letter could be expanded to insure that doctors receive their first information about a new drug from this source rather than from the lips of a detail man.

Let me sum up. Advertising often plays a role analogous to that played by market concentration. We have taken a dim view of excessive concentration precisely because it leads to monopoly results, and this is a major element of the rationale which underlies the laws prohibiting anticompetitive mergers. Current policies which tend to emphasize the role played by concentration may well need to be supplemented by those concerned directly with the adverse influences of advertising and other promotional efforts on competition. We should begin to consider seriously how best we might promote and develop other methods of supplying information to consumers—methods which would give the consumer much better and more useful information than he now gets and at lower social cost; which would thus decrease the impact, profitability, and amount of private advertising expenditures; and which would consequently improve competition in many industries by lowering barriers to entry.

A BUSINESSMAN LOOKS AT CONSUMER PROTECTION [5]

In the *Michigan Law Review*'s "Symposium on Consumer Protection," May 1966, the lead-off article was written by an attorney who holds the position of Special Counsel of the Senate Subcom-

[5] From "The Consumer," an address by Lloyd E. Skinner, president of Skinner Macaroni Company, to the ninth annual Freedom of Information Conference, at the University of Missouri, Columbia, December 6, 1966. *Vital Speeches of the Day.* 33:189-92. Ja. 1, '67. Reprinted by permission.

mittee on Antitrust and Monopoly. Perhaps to some extent we are fortunate that it said "the views expressed are the author's and do not necessarily reflect the opinion of any member of the Subcommittee or any other person on its staff."

The author calls for the establishment of a Federal agency to be called the Consumers Protection Service. So that the consumer "may buy wisely," he asks—

1. that the general characteristics of a product be described by its generic name (the label should state that "Purex" is a "household liquid bleach")
2. where products vary in quality, they should be graded
3. where necessary to avoid deception and to minimize confusion, packages should be standardized in terms of size and, perhaps, container design and
4. a package's physical content and the product's ingredients should be stated in a prominent place on the label (A way to implement this, the author says, is to use the method widely used in Sweden of placing such information—and no other— in a black-bordered square or rectangle occupying not less than 25 per cent of the container's surface area.)

In calling for compulsory adoption of this program, the author explains that consumers must have factual information of this type "and they will not get it if the Government stands on the sidelines while buyers make their purchases under conditions of ignorance and deception."

Use of such intemperate language by the author and similar statements by many other proponents of the "consumer" movement tends to confirm that they have little or no faith or confidence in the American system of free competitive enterprise. . . .

These are not isolated views. The demand for "control" of the manufacturing and distributing process, of advertising, of marketing and merchandising, is growing . . . particularly among some segments of Government personnel. In the final analysis the demands of these people, who do not fundamentally believe in the American Free Enterprise System will only be met by the presence of an all-powerful "Big Brother" who will make the decisions for everyone. They are planting the seeds carrying the destruction of our incentive system of private enterprise all about us. There must be steadfast resistance now.

A Critique of "Consumer Protection"

I hope . . . to develop a sharper focus on the whole area of "consumer protection." The most glaring deficiency about this "movement" is that the total record is replete with personal opinions, unsupported generalities, theories, and obvious prejudice against one or more elements of our marketing system. There is a remarkable absence of cold facts and of competent studies which demonstrate either the need or the practicality of trying to distinguish between protection of the consumer, as such, and protection of the broad public interest. We have in this country literally thousands of regulatory laws, both state and Federal, which directly and indirectly protect the consumer as a primary element of the broad public interest. Of necessity, the administration of these laws has been thoughtfully directed through exclusive and manageable channels—carefully aimed at protection of the public interest whether the objective be furtherance of fair competition, protection of the public health and safety, regulation of transportation, utilities, banking, sale of securities or some other phase of our commerce. . . .

Let me call your attention to the fact there are now within our Federal Government 253 consumer protective agencies. Is that enough? Should they all be placed into one gigantic bureau? Well, here is what Paul Rand Dixon, Chairman of the Federal Trade Commission, told a group of advertising executives in New York . . . when asked for his views on a Consumer Department at Cabinet level. He was opposed to it and said, "All of us are supposed to represent the public and we're all consumers. The consumer is pretty well represented in the United States Government now. . . .

The so-called consumer movement, which has been portrayed as a demand by an "impatient public," is to a very great extent stimulated by those people in government who seek to control business. During the time the so-called truth-in-packaging bill was under consideration, my home city of Omaha was visited on two different occasions by members of the staff of the President's Adviser on Consumer Affairs for the purpose of organizing a Consumer League. They were brazen enough to hold their first meeting in the United Community Services building and, of course, with the inference that it had the UCS blessings. Their attempts at organization failed in both instances when it became apparent that endorsement of the packaging bill was the real purpose of the meetings.

Of course, if they had succeeded, our congressman would have received a wire from the newly formed Omaha Consumer League insisting he vote favorably on the packaging bill.

The general tone that surrounds any discussion of "the consumer's right to know" appears to cast industry on the one hand and consumers on the other in roles which are basically antagonistic and incompatible. This is certainly not a realistic view, and in fact grossly misrepresents the attitude of the food manufacturer. The truth is that the patronage of consumers is absolutely essential to the success of our business—but this patronage hinges on a number of factors which include price, quality, packaging, class of advertising, class of distribution, manner of display, type of promotion, and the general reputation of the product. . . .

The Business of Business

In addition to these considerations, it must be remembered that the paramount consideration of any business enterprise is to stay in business and there are a great many concerns in the food industry with high quality competitive products which have exactly the same idea. I would venture to assert that well over 95 per cent of the huge volume of food items sold in this country today are beyond serious criticism with respect to display of price and weight, and general packaging practice. The competition between brands is so keen that no manufacturer wants to risk losing a sale because of the failure of his product to give the consumer the facts. It is in the manufacturer's own self-interest to give information to the consumer, not only to motivate the initial sale, but to cultivate that customer so that the product will be bought again, and again, and again. You cannot stay in business long on initial purchases. It is the repeat business, some call it "good will" for the product, that is the foundation for success in the manufacturing business.

For example, we may come up with a new product which is sold to the consumer for 39 cents. The true cost for putting the first package of that product on the shelf could be many thousands of dollars. To bring that product to the marketplace, the manufacturer must make a heavy investment: in marketing studies; in the purchase of raw materials; in human energy and machinery and equipment to produce, package, label and distribute it. He risks that heavy investment because of confidence he has made a product that will appeal to the consumer and give the consumer satisfaction. If he is wrong, there will be no repeat business and for all practical purposes that investment is money thrown out the window. For every product success in the marketplace, there are hundreds of failures. It is obvious that self-interest requires the manufacturer to be in the consumer's camp. He must have the consumer's vote of approval, and election day for the manufacturer is every day.

There is no room for mistakes in our business. Lack of knowledge of the market, ignorance of cost factors, and unawareness of the competitive pressures can put us out of business as quickly as anything I know, and yet it has been seriously proposed to give Government bureaucracy control over many of the vital decisions necessary to marketing.

By way of example, consider the much-discussed issue of the packaging bill. The law as finally enacted in this past session of Congress differs considerably from the bill originally passed by the Senate. The Senate version provided for mandatory packaging standards. The Senate bill gave the Federal Trade Commission or the Secretary of Health, Education, and Welfare the power to issue package size standards. The standards could have been made mandatory by the Agency's adoption of them. A "gun-in-the-back" provision permitted industry to avoid the standards issued by the Government agencies by adoption of voluntary standards under Department of Commerce procedures.

This law is symbolic of unwarranted governmental intrusion into, and unnecessary interference with, the working of the market-place. This proposed packaging law did not deal with offenses which as a matter of public policy ought to be prohibited by general law. It dealt with matters of personal opinion—about what kind of information can be easily understood by a consumer of the lowest mentality. The implication of Government witnesses and other professional consumer groups, who testified on this bill was that the average consumer is a fool with the mental perception of a backward child. Surely you will agree this is not the case.

When the Government becomes involved in the marketplace, the inevitable result is pressure on the marketing and communications system of the manufacturer. This can result in disastrous expenses for a small firm. Anyone who has ever had experience with Government knows that to obtain Government approval on almost any question entails six months' to a year's delay, to say nothing of the expenditure of many thousands of dollars in trying to convince some official of the necessity of doing things in a particular way—whether it be to meet competition, to satisfy the psychological preferences of the consumers, to reduce manufacturing costs, or staying within the performance limits of automated machinery.

I wonder if anyone has stopped to think that the idea of seeking Government authority in advance before making a vital business decision is absolutely inconsistent with some of our most fundamental and cherished American traditions. Advance government permission is the Latin system—nothing can be done without a government license. Unless I have been misinformed all these years, I have been under the impression that in this country we are dedicated to the proposition that, within reasonable limitations, the American citizen is free to do as he pleases, and that if he transgresses the law he must be tried and proved guilty of a specific offense.

There has been, and there will continue to be, pressure from Federal, state and local governments to deal with merchandising ethics which are matters purely subject to personal opinion. What kind of adjectives will be regarded as likely to mislead? What kind of pictorial matter leads to a false conclusion about the product?

What is a proper relation of price to weight? How full is a full pack when you produce a number of food products of different densities and shapes which inevitably will settle and reduce in volume as a consequence of transportation? Furthermore, it certainly cannot be argued that these considerations are of such gravity that public policy demands advance clearance by the Government. Such a contention would be little short of ridiculous.

The Problem of Small Firms

Any involvement by Government in the mechanics of our marketing and distribution system would make it even more difficult for the small firm to be competitive and thus to retain its share of the market. The impact of such interference unquestionably is greater on the small firm because it forces higher costs. For example, should mandatory packaging standards be set by any governmental body, the ability of major firms to retool or purchase machinery or equipment is related to their ability to finance such retooling and purchases. The smaller firm on the other hand, and especially in light of today's tight money market would be seriously handicapped, and unable to retool in time to maintain even its small position in the industry. The result would be a higher concentration of business among a relatively few, large companies.

My own company by any standard is a relatively small business. Yet we produce macaroni products in nineteen or twenty different shapes. We buy cases and cartons cheaper because of our standardization by dimensions. For example, in standardizing by dimension and density, we are able to have many products packed in the same size package and case. If the Senate version of the packaging bill requiring standardization by weight would have passed, we would have been required to produce many new-size packages.

We presently have about $300,000 invested in packaging equipment. We would have been forced to have spent $86,000 more for new packaging machines, and an expansion of our plant facilities to accommodate the new machines would have cost another $100,000.

Another cost factor in the production of a consumer product is the "down time" of these packaging machines. Our packaging machines presently operate about 90 per cent of the time. If we had been forced to add the additional machines, we would have found that they would operate only about 40 to 50 per cent of the time. For these reasons, our cost of producing macaroni would have increased somewhere between 1 cent and 2 cents per package.

I think it is obvious: that big consumer protection programs are neither desirable nor necessary; that such programs would increase the cost of products for the consumer; that consumer protection bureaucracies would make it more difficult for the small firms to operate or even stay in business; and that cost of these huge Government bureaucracies would represent another burden for the consumer and the taxpayer.

I submit that there is no magic (except for purely political purposes) in the word *consumer*. Protection of the public interest has encompassed the protection of buyers. Our antitrust laws and the FTC Act were passed primarily for the benefit of ultimate purchasers. I have yet to see a factual delineation of any area in which the American "consumer" is disadvantaged in any manner to a degree which justifies, as a matter of public policy, the stupendous costs of bureaucracy to consumers and to taxpayers.

I say to you, private industry working in a competitive atmosphere under our free enterprise system is delivering to the American consumer a far better value for his dollar and higher standard of living than the world has ever before known. Let's keep it that way.

Let our commerce continue to operate with the absolute minimum of Government control and regulation.

IV. CONSUMER CONCERNS

EDITOR'S INTRODUCTION

Although many specific consumer problems are dealt with throughout this compilation, those discussed in this section are currently in the limelight and may well be attacked next through new legislation or other Government action. (See "Current Presidential Proposals," in Section II, above.)

That "the poor pay more" was vaguely understood long before the "war on poverty," but the problem has recently been explored in depth. In our complex economy many of the needs of the low-income consumer relate to high-priced housing, health requirements, and a vast array of commodities for home and personal use. With installment buying have come credit schemes that are at best not fully comprehensible and at worst fraudulent. All of these questions are dealt with in the selection by David Caplovitz, author of the book *The Poor Pay More.*

A report on the annoying problem, often with fraudulence built in, of faulty parts and deceptive business practices is given by Isadore Barmash of the New York *Times* staff. Questions about the cost of medical care are covered in a report to the President by the Consumer Advisory Council. The new interest in automobile insurance as a consumer problem and one that is also gravely overloading our courts is discussed in a *Time* magazine essay and by Jeffrey O'Connell, a professor of law at the University of Illinois. The author offers a plan which would give far more immediate benefits to victims of auto accidents and might rid the courts of much accident litigation.

The section concludes with two items on consumer problems relating to radiation from TV sets and the need for regulation of seafood processing and distribution and an inquiry into a wholly new confrontation between the consumer and the marketing mechanism. Lee Kanner, a reporter for the New York *Times*, finds that with the introduction of computer systems to take care of customer-seller transactions, credit, and payment responses, the customer often encounters nonresponse, a new consumer woe.

CONSUMER PROBLEMS OF THE POOR [1]

My remarks will bear upon the problems that low-income persons face as consumers in our society. Until recently the "war on poverty" was focused exclusively on the earning power of the poor and how to expand it through education, job training and creation of jobs. But the inability of the poor to earn a decent living is only one side of their economic plight. Equally important is how the poor spend what little income they have, that is, their situation as consumers making major buying decisions in the marketplace. To the extent that the poor pay more for the goods they buy—and I am convinced that they do—then to that extent they are deprived of the benefits of their earning power. They are forced to live in a world of inflation that our more well-to-do citizens are able to escape.

The Lure of Installment Buying

The tendency has been to assume that, since the poor have little money to spend, they cannot possibly be consumers of costly merchandise. But this reasoning overlooks the role of installment credit in our society. Through the mass media, Americans in all walks of life are bombarded with messages to buy now and pay later. "Easy payments" and "no money down" are the slogans luring even the poor into the marketplace. Nor is it very difficult to lure the poor into making costly purchases, for in some ways the ownership of goods takes on even more significance for low-income persons than for those in higher income brackets. Since the poor have little prospect of greatly improving their local social standing through occupational mobility, they are apt to turn to consumption as at least one sphere in which they can make some progress toward

[1] From an address delivered at the New York Consumer Assembly, January 14, 1967, by David Caplovitz, adjunct professor of sociology at Columbia University, associated with the University's Bureau of Applied Social Research, and author of *The Poor Pay More. Co-Op Contact* (publication of the United Housing Foundation). p CC7+. Spring '67. Reprinted by permission.

the American dream of success. Appliances, automobiles and the dream of a home of their own can become compensations for blocked social mobility.

Whatever the motive, there is increasing evidence that the poor are consumers of major durables. My own study of almost five hundred low-income families, living in public housing projects in New York City, showed that these families owned many expensive appliances. Fully 95 per cent owned at least one television set; almost two thirds owned a phonograph; almost half owned a sewing machine and almost half owned an automatic washing machine. Most of these families had spent considerable money furnishing their apartments. The typical family bought sets of furniture for at least two rooms when it moved into public housing and had spent approximately $500 for furniture. Some 16 per cent had paid more than $1,000 for furniture bought at the time of the move.

The prices they paid for appliances were quite high. Forty per cent paid more than $300 for their TV set and 13 per cent had paid more than $400. A number of families owned expensive combination television and phonograph sets and one family reported paying $900 for such an appliance.

Partly because they are so dependent upon credit and partly because they are intimidated by the large downtown store, most of the families buy their major durables from neighborhood merchants or from door-to-door peddlers rather than going to the large department stores and discount houses. Symbolic of the narrow shopping scope of the poor is the practice of buying from door-to-door peddlers, the men with the traditional slogan of "a dollar down, a dollar a week." Fully half the families surveyed had made at least one credit purchase from these door-to-door salesmen and more than a third had made repeated purchases.

The poor, then, like others in our society, have major wants as consumers, and there are innumerable merchants in low-income areas who are all too eager to provide them with the goods they want (and I might add, often with goods that they do not want).

Prey to Unscrupulous Salesmen

Because they are poor and have such low ratings as credit risks and because they lack the training to be sophisticated shoppers, persons of low income are easy prey to unscrupulous, exploitative merchants. The marketing system in which they are forced to operate is in many respects a deviant system. I have elsewhere described it as a commercial jungle in which exploitation and fraud are the norm rather than the exception. High pressure tactics, "bait" ads and "switch sales," misrepresentation of price and quality, and the sale of used merchandise as new all flourish in this special system of sales-and-credit. Responding to ads announcing appliances and furniture at unusually low prices, the consumer soon succumbs to the salesman's switch-sale technique and buys a much more expensive model. . . .

I could go on and illustrate many other exploitative practices that are used to bilk the poor, such as the promise of free merchandise if the consumer will assist the salesman in finding other customers, extravagant verbal promises that prove to have no validity, or the delivery of merchandise other than that ordered, but by now, these exploitative schemes are all too well known. . . .

Perhaps less well known is that there are even salesmen who specialize in extending credit to families who are on welfare. Last year I learned about two cases that had come to the legal office of Mobilization for Youth in New York City. In both instances, women on welfare were talked into buying expensive television sets. The salesman said he would be by every two weeks when the welfare check came to collect $10. They were told that the sets would cost $200 but when they were delivered, the women discovered that they had to pay $600. In spite of the suddenly inflated price of the merchandise, these women kept up payments until their sets broke down and the company refused to make repairs in spite of guarantees that they had been given. Their withholding of payments led to their sets being repossessed and it was only at that time that they sought legal aid.

Faulty Merchandise

These incidents illustrate another point that must be made. Many poor people find themselves overextended in credit obligations and unable to maintain payments. But many others stop paying on their purchases not because they are unable to pay, but because they refuse to pay on faulty merchandise. Instead of . . . [being reimbursed], however, they are more often than not subjected to legal sanctions brought upon them by the merchant. . . .

I should point out that the jungle confronting the poor consumer extends to the procedural aspects of the law. Legal procedures are violated with some frequency by the merchants' attorneys and the city marshals who are responsible for collecting the debts.

For example, almost all the lawsuits against consumers who do not pay result in judgments by default, that is, the consumers do not show up in court to defend themselves. The assumption commonly made is that these default judgments simply mean that the consumer has no case; that he indeed owes the money and therefore chooses not to answer the complaint and risk further court costs. But the legal unit of Mobilization for Youth has come across a number of cases in which the defendant was never served with a summons. Process servers often evade their responsibility and simply throw the summons away. This happens with sufficient frequency that a special term has evolved in legal circles to refer to it: "sewer service." Low-income families are especially likely to be victims of this practice since they are not apt to know their legal rights or how to protect them. . . .

Alternatives Needed

It is all too easy to say that the poor must be educated as consumers. But in my opinion, it is even more important to provide the poor with meaningful alternatives to the present arrangements that confront them. I have in mind such things as credit unions, cooperatives and other self-help institutions.

In addition, there is a need for new legislation that will redress the balance between creditors' rights and debtors' rights. For example, we take pride in the fact that debtors' prisons have been abolished and yet today our legal structure permits garnishments which often result in depriving the debtor of his livelihood. Fortunately, . . . New York State has finally passed a law prohibiting employers from firing workers for this reason.

Until recently, I thought losing a job because of a garnishment order was the worst thing that could happen to the low-income consumer. But then I learned something about how the system works in the state of Pennsylvania. Pennsylvania is one of the few states in the country in which garnishment of wages is not permitted—an eminently desired state of affairs. But, in Pennsylvania, it is very easy for the creditor to attach the property of the debtor. Many working-class people who have managed to buy their homes find themselves losing title to their houses because of their installment debts. Every month, hundreds of houses in Philadelphia are sold at sheriffs' auctions for a small fraction of their value to settle consumer debts.

Certainly truth-in-lending legislation is necessary if consumers are to behave rationally. We urge consumers to shop wisely and yet we tolerate a situation in which it is virtually impossible for consumers to shop for credit for the simple reason that those who extend credit are not required to state how much the credit costs. The variations in credit legislation from state to state are not only awesome but difficult to justify. For example, in the state of Arkansas, the maximum interest that can be charged on any loan is 10 per cent, but the State of Texas permits over 200 per cent interest on loans under $100.

Merchants Have Problems, Too

I should now like to say a word on behalf of those I have treated as the villains, the local merchants in poverty areas. In my opinion, it is a mistake to see their practices as wholly due to . . . [unscrupulousness]. They, too, are constrained by a set of economic forces. In some respects these merchants must charge more for the simple reason that it costs them more to operate. I am not thinking only of the fact that being small businessmen, they cannot buy in bulk the way chain stores or large department stores can. I also have in mind the fact that these merchants frequently have to pay more for the money they borrow and in particular that they have to pay more for the insurance they need. If I am not mistaken, the insurance companies of America are now facing a crisis concerning insurance in ghetto areas. Even at the much higher rates they charge, they apparently are not finding it profitable to extend insurance to ghetto merchants. There is need, then, for new institutional arrangements to meet the needs of the local merchant as well as those of the local consumer. Why, for example, can not there be some system of pooling insurance and sharing the risk so that the local merchant does not have to pay an exorbitant price for insurance?

Moreover, the merchant whose business is located in the ghetto is far from being the most evil person in the system of exploitation of the poor. To some extent his practices are constrained by the need to maintain "good will" with his customers. Much more despicable, I think, are the fly-by-night companies which send their canvassers into the ghetto to sell such expensive commodities as encyclopedias, pots and pans, deep freezers and vacuum cleaners. These companies specialize in sharp practices. Once they make their dishonest sales they quickly sell their paper to finance companies and benefit from the immunity that the law now gives them from further responsibility for the sale.

And I should point out that these disreputable companies could not long survive without the collusion of the equally disreputable finance companies and banks which buy their paper. These financial institutions must share the blame for the exploitation of the poor, for they know all too well that they are buying "bad" paper, that is, dishonestly obtained contracts, and yet they do so anyway. And when we ask the further question of where the finance companies get the funds that they need to operate, we soon discover that they often borrow from highly respectable banks. Thus, the so-called respectable financial community is also a party to the exploitation of the poor.

A Note of Optimism

I should like to close on a note of optimism. Earlier, I mentioned the need for self-help institutions to protect the interests of low-income consumers. We hear a good deal these days about the great difficulty of organizing the poor to take action on the problems that face them. But recently I learned about an organization that has restored my confidence in the power of the poor. This organization is located in Philadelphia and is called the Consumer Education and Protective Association. CEPA was formed about eight months ago and today [in the spring of 1967] has about five hundred members. It operates on a shoestring. Through membership dues and contributions they have managed to raise $5,000. And what have they accomplished? By using the union weapon of the picket line, they have forced many merchants to make refunds on unconscionable transactions. A key to their success is a monthly newspaper that they distribute in the low-income areas. Their paper is called "Consumers Voice" and their slogan is "Let the Seller Beware." . . . Their accomplishments can be seen from the headlines. For example, one headline reads, "Pickets at N.Y. Bank Stop Sheriff Sale"; another announces, "Finance Co. Refunds $730"; and another says, "Dealer Takes Back $3,000 Used Car."

This organization has become so effective that the opposition is beginning to organize to shoot them down. Soon they will be sued for unauthorized practice of law. But my guess is that they have sufficiently aroused the low-income population of Philadelphia so that they will not easily be put out of business. I think that we here in New York have much to learn from CEPA, and would do well to develop a similar organization. Through such efforts and through more effective legislation, the day may come when the poor are given a fair shake in the marketplace.

FAULTY PARTS AND FRAUDULENT PRACTICES [2]

A New Jersey resident needed a new tailpipe for his automobile and gave the job to a local mechanic for an agreed-upon sum of $20.

[2] From "Legislators Study Bills on Abuses," by Isadore Barmash, staff reporter on business news. New York *Times.* p 1F+. N. 12, '67. © 1967 by The New York Times Company. Reprinted by permission.

When he returned to pick up the three-year-old car, he was presented with a bill for $40, also covering a repair on the motor he had not requested. Of course, he complained and the station owner reluctantly agreed to split the difference to $30.

A New Yorker almost immediately began to have problems with a new $500 color television set. On the third service call, he was told: "You've got a problem with an 'intermittent tube.' When it stops working, just tap it with a wooden spoon."

The set's owner knew that this was contrary to the precaution usually furnished by the manufacturer that the layman shouldn't tamper with a set. He wrote a bitter letter to the president of the company that made the set. Six months after he made the purchase, he got a new picture tube.

Recently, a Queens salesman began wondering if he shouldn't consult a psychiatrist. Every time he drove his car, he thought it was raining. He clearly heard the sound of gurgling water, but no rain was falling.

Finally, one day, he listened closely to his steering wheel and headed frantically for the nearest service station. It seemed that the car's steering column was full of water, which had apparently accumulated from both condensation and a leakage. The mechanic told him it was the first time that he had ever run into such a problem.

Many Such Incidents

Although these are merely random incidents of consumer problems with servicing and faulty products, such stories are legion. But the sharply-increasing occurrence of such incidents is now becoming a national issue, creating not only headlines and threats of legislative curbs in many cities but reaching to the White House through letters from disturbed consumers.

In California, the state has acted to curb repair abuses by compelling television repair shops to register at an annual $35 fee and comply with a set of rules aimed to tell the consumer exactly what was done.

In New York, the city's license commissioner, Joel J. Tyler, said recently that his agency was preparing proposed legislation for licensing television repairmen.

Also, in New York . . . the City Council Committee on General Welfare heard Lewis B. Scott, director of research for the Automobile Club of New York, advocate legislation that would "eliminate the unconscionable practices" of charging for repairs not actually made, replacing parts that are in good working order and charging new-part prices for rebuilt parts.

Since 1962, the New York State Automobile Association has gone on record in support of state legislation to correct fraudulent practices associated with the repair of motor vehicles. For four years, Senator Edward J. Speno, Republican of Nassau [county], has supported legislation that would license repair shops throughout the state. Two licensing bills are pending.

Urgent Action Sought

Mr. Tyler, city licensing commissioner, also has announced that his department has uncovered "widespread abuse" by used-car salesmen and was preparing legislation to license them.

In the face of rising rates for service calls recently put into effect by the large producers of television sets, evidence of tricksters' "conning" consumers on TV receivers was recently disclosed by Illinois' attorney general William Clark.

He learned that some repairmen were charging $14.85 to $45.70 for repairing sets in which all that was needed was the replacement of one or two tubes, at an actual cost of $5 to $15.

What is behind the problem?

Is the age of affluence and more sophisticated technology creating two-car families and three-television-set homes while at the same time diminishing the appeal of the technician or serviceman because he can earn more elsewhere and do less? . . .

Consumer complaints that reach the White House are about equally divided on the servicing and repairs of both automobiles and appliances.

When I refer to the greatest percentage of mail that I get involving public frustration with servicing problems [said Betty Furness, special assistant to the President for consumer affiairs], I have to lump the two areas of autos and appliances. And while the letters also complain on prices, the writers apparently would be happy just to have the repairs done properly.

Concern Indicated

The fading days of the franchise system of distribution are contributing to the problem, Miss Furness believes, explaining that when appliance dealers concentrated on only one or perhaps two lines, "they and their servicemen knew the products in the line." But today, she added, the ambitious opening up of distribution pipelines is creating a lack of knowledge of the servicing end of the appliance business.

In one sense, she said, this situation is typified by store salesmen, who, when asked for information about features of an appliance, answer: "Lady, here's the circular. It gives you the information."

Today, she added, retail salespeople don't seem to know as much about merchandise as their predecessors did. Either they are not as well educated, or they do not have the opportunity, Miss Furness stated.

The General Electric Company was cited by the presidential assistant both favorably and unfavorably. "G.E. has service centers for appliances in the big cities," she said. "They at least do that. But what about the small cities? There are lots of consumers living there, too."

She said that she has not contacted the automobile industry to pass on the complaints she has received on auto servicing. However, she believes that the Consumer Advisory Council of the Department of Commerce may do this, and, in addition, may take up the matter of appliance repairs.

In commenting on Miss Furness's remarks, the staff executive of the 7,000-member National Radio and Appliance Dealers Association in Chicago declared that "by the very nature of her job, Miss Furness cannot be aware of the 'nonproblems' of consumers in relation to the merchandise they buy. Unfortunately, consumers do not write to pass on compliments." . . .

Study Conducted

In an attempt to overcome the shortage of technicians, the Association has conducted a study of service complaints in Indiana and determined that about 80 per cent of the failures of machines are contributed to by less than a dozen causes. The appliance dealers' group is now using these findings to explore methods of increasing the availability of service technicians, said Mr. [Jules] Steinberg [executive vice president of the Association].

By isolating the most common causes, he said, it will be possible, as a short-term solution, to develop less-qualified technicians from an available labor supply. Such potential servicemen might be school dropouts or others less qualified by education than the professional technician.

However, more important will be such long-range aids as the development of training schools. This effort is being pursued by the dealers' group with both the Association of Home Appliance Manufacturers and the manpower development department of the Department of Commerce, he said.

Miss Furness and . . . [New York City's] licensing bills on automotive repairmen came under fire last week from Mac Victor, executive director of the Inter-City Service Stations Association. The trade group consists of six hundred service stations in Manhattan, the Bronx, Staten Island and Westchester County.

When Miss Furness refers to high prices for repairs [he said], she cannot seriously mean that auto service bills are high when the work is done by service stations. Our prices per hour are lower than those for other technical crafts. In auto repairs, the labor charge is $7 an hour. This compares with $15 an hour for electrical workers and comparative high rates for carpenters and plumbers. . . .

Constant Use a Factor

Car owners are resentful over repair costs because owning an auto is an expensive item. . . . However, many people forget that repair costs are nothing more than paying for the maintenance of a machine that is virtually in constant use and so suffers wear and tear, Mr. Victor said.

"There is no question that the main problem is the lack of young people to come into the automotive service industry," declared a spokesman for Local 917 of the Teamsters' Union, an affiliate of the International Brotherhood of Teamsters. "There is little glamour that we can offer them and younger people don't like to dirty their hands like their forebears did," he added.

The New York Teamsters' local, whose members include service station employees, offered this comparison of wages: Service station attendants, $70-$90 a week; service station mechanics, $105 to $130 a week; truck rental mechanics, $146.40 for a forty-hour week, and auto mechanics in the construction industry, $201.20 for a forty-hour week.

THE CONSUMER AND HEALTH SERVICES [3]

The consumer is often beset by many uncertainties in securing health care. He has little direction in the selection of a physician. Furthermore, he is not usually in a position to "shop and compare" as in purchasing automobiles and other consumer commodities. When he needs a physician, he often needs one fast because he is either ill or believes he is. In addition, as a layman, he is in a poor position to evaluate the ability or the dedication of physicians. And his alternatives in the purchase of health care are often narrow. He must take what is available at a particular time, in a particular city.

The present generation has witnessed a revolutionary change in public attitudes toward health. Once considered the exclusive concern of the physician in the privacy of his office or the hospital room, the protection of human health is now viewed as a responsibility of many individuals, professions, private agencies, and government agencies.

A striking index of this national concern is the rising proportion of the Gross National Product spent for health—from 4.5 per cent in 1950 to 5.8 per cent in 1964. It is estimated that in 1964, $36.8 billion was spent by all sources for all health services. The Federal

[3] From "Health Services," a report. In Consumer Advisory Council. *Consumer Issues '66; a Report to the President.* General Services Administration. Washington. D.C. 20405. '66. p 79-91.

Government alone spent $4.8 billion. Thus, the health of the consumer in the United States is the focus of a gigantic effort. Roughly 2.4 million persons are employed directly in the "health industry."

This expansion in expenditures, personnel and policy points up a growing acceptance of the view that good health is a right not a privilege, and a right not to be abridged by circumstance of birth or by ability to pay.

In the words of President Johnson:

Adequate health protection and medical care once were considered privileges in America: privileges limited to those who could afford the best. Today our nation has greater wealth and a greater heart. We are learning to think of good health not as a privilege for the few, but as a basic right for all. . . .

The ability to pay, perhaps more than any single factor, limits the capacity of millions of consumers to exercise fully their right to good health. Poverty chains man to his environment—and to the substandard health care which is part of the cycle of deprivation.

Paradoxes bedevil present-day health care. Medical science has won a major victory over many communicable diseases, yet millions of Americans are unable to afford the care made possible by the research laboratories. Techniques of higher quality care are possible, yet the organization and delivery of the care to the consumer are often inefficient and wasteful. Great attention is given to pharmaceuticals and therapeutics, yet little attention is paid to prevention.

Basic Economics of Health Care

Good health care is not cheap. In 1964, the last full year for which data are available, per capita expenditures for health by all sources—private and governmental—amounted to $191.

Private sources spent approximately 75 per cent of the total national outlay of $36.8 billion. Of this amount, almost 68 per cent came from consumers, either directly or through insurance. Federal and state government accounted for the remaining 25 per cent.

Almost 91 per cent of the national expenditures in 1964 was spent for health services and supplies, and only $3.3 billion was allocated for medical research and the construction of hospitals and related facilities.

Not only has the amount of spending trebled between 1950 and 1964, but also the proportion of the health dollar expended for hospitals, nursing home care, and research has increased. In contrast, the share spent for the services of professional personnel in private practice and for medical supplies declined.

Only $7.8 billion, or one third of the $23.7 billion expended by consumers for personal health care in 1964, was paid through health insurance. The balance, $15.9 billion, represented direct out-of-pocket consumer payments for such care.

As the nation increases its capacity to preserve health and cure disease, it faces rising costs of health services and care, and short supplies of facilities and skilled personnel.

Application of today's new knowledge requires an almost unbelievable array of complex, expensive equipment and facilities for diagnosis and treatment. As the knowledge increases, so, correspondingly, do the required services in health care.

Artificial kidneys, more sophisticated heart-lung machines, the prospect of replacing part of the human heart, advanced X-ray procedures—all exciting developments in the science of medicine—necessitate new thinking in the economics of medicine.

The consumer rightfully expects to receive the fruits of medical science, and he cannot be entirely blamed for the shock he experiences when he is presented his bill on leaving the hospital. The reasons for such high costs have never been explained in terms he can comprehend.

Need for More and Better Health Personnel

The high cost of illness is explainable not only in terms of equipment, gadgetry, and facilities, but also in terms of scarce manpower. As medical care has become more effective, it has grown more complex, fragmented and impersonal. Inevitably the medical profession has specialized. Groups of supporting experts—chemists, therapists, electronics experts, radiation physicists, nutritionists—are now required in the health industry....

Clearly there is a need for improved organization of health services in order to provide the consumer with the most efficient

form of health care. The day is long past when any single physician—no matter how talented—can hope to give his patients the
best of all medical care in all areas of medicine.

Consequently, the last forty years—and particularly since 1946
—have witnessed the rise and growth of various forms of group
practice, and a progressive decline in the number, availability and
professional status of family physicians. The concept of pooling
professional skills for mutual benefit has appealed to thousands of
physicians. Medical group practice combined with prepayment
has been stimulated by labor unions and consumer groups.

Group practice tends to counteract the fragmentation which
results from specialization and, in a very practical sense, group
practice tends to make readily available family-type medical
care. . . .

Medicare—The Historic Turning Point

Medicare legislation stands as a historic turning point in the
long struggle to improve personal health service in the United
States. It provides the nation with a new principle, and a new
opportunity full of meaning for the average consumer.

For more than twenty years, the national debate on health
services has focused on the philosophical question of whether the
principle of social insurance or voluntary insurance should prevail.
This debate, though consonant with the democratic process, served
to confuse many other important issues in comprehensive health
care. Even some of the advocates of social insurance were sometimes hesitant about bringing important gaps in our health services
into the discussion for fear of "rocking the social insurance boat,"
so to speak. . . .

Enactment of Medicare offers new opportunity to develop a rational integrated system of health services for the consumer. However, the full protection of the consumer under Medicare, as under
many other laws of such magnitude, requires continuous surveil-
lance and review.

Since it is natural in the legislative process to adopt certain
compromises, it will be necessary to reexamine details of Medicare,
especially limitations of coverage and financing, which were

adopted in the stress and strain of bringing the legislation to a vote before Congress.

The extensive dialogue, among government, groups representing the health industry, and consumers, which has taken place since enactment of Medicare, makes clear that some adjustment of operating details will be necessary to protect the consumer against some of the economic practices of the past which the law was designed to overcome.

One of the most necessary changes is to eliminate deductibles and coinsurance provisions from Medicare. Both deductibles and coinsurance represent economic and administrative barriers to the full application of the social insurance principle and, in fact, dilute the principle and the purpose of the law.

Deductibles may prevent some consumers from obtaining health care when they need it. Medicare's exclusion of preventive care in the absence of overt illness compounds the illogical limitation. Coinsurance may impose harsh alternatives on the consumer either by leaving him with a substantial unpaid bill after treatment, or by forcing him to forgo some types of care as he cannot afford the cost.

The only justification for inclusion of deductibles and coinsurance and exclusion of preventive services from Medicare is that they limit the demands on the Social Security Trust Funds by requiring the user of services to share the cost. However, the cost of administering these complex provisions reduces the financial saving they make to the Trust Funds.

The insurance industry is offering a variety of supplemental insurance programs to fill in the gaps in Medicare's coverage. However, consumers and government should be alert to the need to protect the aged from buying insurance which is inadequate and costly. Moreover, it is urgently necessary to give all consumers simple explanations of the true value and meaning, down to the policy's fine print, of the health insurance they purchase.

Even with Medicare, the insurance protection of all consumers will not be fully achieved under insurance industry's present "experience rating." Competitive underwriting selects the good risk groups for economical, closely calculated premiums, and leaves the poorer risks exposed to premiums which eventually price them out of the market. Witness, for example, the situation of the elderly which made Medicare inevitable.

This inherent characteristic of voluntary insurance, combined with the fragmented systems for providing personal health services that have evolved under our *laissez-faire* approach to hospitals, specialist services, and fee-for-service method of paying for medical care call urgently for expanded action to improve both organization and financing.

Indeed, the social insurance principle itself should be extended to certain population groups now excluded and who may be in the most critical need for the services the new law offers. The history of Social Security legislation in the United States, entailing a consistent extension of benefits from an initial small operating base, provides a pattern for a similar extension of Medicare. Planning should begin now for such an anticipated extension. . . .

In private health insurance plans, "experience rating" techniques, which in effect increase the premiums of groups which require health services the most, should be replaced with a community rating system enabling an entire enrolled population to share the risks.

Group Practice—An Important Alternative

Dr. George Baehr of New York City, a noted internist and one of the nation's distinguished medical administrators, summed up the shortcomings of solo practices on a fee-for-service basis:

Athough voluntary health insurance has indeed prospered and is now being sold to over 145 million persons by more than 1,800 individual insurance carriers, their fee-for-service indemnity payments do not defray more than 30 per cent of the total cost of family medical care, if one includes the costs of hospitalization, physicians' and dentists' services, drugs and medical appliances, nursing and other paramedical services required for the care of the sick and the prevention of illness.

After thirty-three years, comprehensive coverage for the costs of medical care still remains largely uninsurable for the simple reason that the predominant pattern of private medical practice continues to be solo practice on a fee-for-service basis as it was one hundred years ago.

The limitations of solo fee-for-service arrangements give rise to the corollary question: Is a better system available?

The answer is yes, in group practice of medicine. Group practice takes many forms, from an informal association of two or more physicians to the formalized structure of a group health plan, such as the Health Insurance Plan of Greater New York and the Kaiser Foundation Health Plan in the West, which offer comprehensive prepaid direct-service care to their members and are financed by capitation charges. . . .

Because group practice plans efficiently organize family physicians, specialists, and supporting personnel into an integrated team, and because they use the capitation method of prepayment for medical care, they are able to provide insured families with comprehensive medical services—preventive and therapeutic—of uniformly high quality. At the same time, they have succeeded in keeping rising costs of family medical care within reasonable limits.

In addition, experience has demonstrated that the need for hospitalization is sharply reduced under group practice plans insofar as consumers have available the unlimited services of family physicians, pediatricians, other specialists, as well as laboratory, X-ray, and ancillary facilities, all located in the same center. . . .

Accessibility of services is another unique advantage of group practice. Contrast such centralized services, for example, with the vexations of an individual in New York City who must travel from specialist to specialist over vast distances for the same services he would receive—at far less cost—in one group practice facility.

For these and other reasons, the increasing enrollment of consumers in prepaid group practice plans, and the establishment of new plans in areas where they do not exist, would represent a significant forward step in enhancing the quality, efficiency and availability of medical care and in limiting its cost.

THE PROBLEM OF AUTO INSURANCE [4]

The grim statistics of highway travel in the world's most motorized society add up to an irresistible sales pitch for auto insurance. Cars have killed more Americans since 1900 than the death toll of

[4] Essay, "The Business With 103 Million Unsatisfied Customers." *Time.* 91:20-1. Ja. 26, '68. Reprinted by permission from TIME, the weekly news magazine; copyright Time Inc. 1968.

all U.S. wars since 1775. Roughly 24 million cars crashed in 1966 alone, injuring 4 million people, disabling 1.9 million and killing 53,000.

The economic loss caused by this carnage is well over $12 billion a year, and there is no question that the United States desperately needs a highly effective auto-insurance system that would compensate traffic victims rapidly, fairly and at reasonable cost to policyholders. But there is no question, either, that the U.S. auto-insurance system is a model of expensive inefficiency. The country's 103 million drivers have every reason to complain.

In ten years, the average premium has soared 55 per cent. Car owners who take out a standard 50/100/5 liability policy (on which the company will pay up to $50,000 to one injured person, a total of up to $100,000 to all persons injured in one accident, and up to $5,000 for property damage) are also likely to include comprehensive protection (fire, theft, etc.), plus a collision policy requiring them to pay the first $100 in repairs. In Los Angeles five years ago, that package cost $279 a year for a couple with an eighteen-year-old son, even though his high school driving course got them a 10 per cent discount and he used their low-priced car for pleasure only. Today the cost is $342—up 23 per cent. In Houston, the rate has risen 49 per cent, to $284.40. Boston tops the United States with a yearly premium of $711—up 71 per cent.

The price of auto insurance is so high that most people would like to find a way of passing it up. But even though New York, Massachusetts and North Carolina are the only states that make liability coverage compulsory, it is virtually unavoidable everywhere. An uninsured driver must buy it or post equivalent financial security as soon as he is involved in a serious accident or gets convicted of a serious driving offense. And whichever alternative he chooses, he is in trouble. With a damage claim hanging over his head, few if any insurers will accept him as a future risk. If he posts personal security, he may lose his home or savings.

Paint It Red

Insurance companies say they are losing their savings, too. Despite the steep rise in premiums, the industry colors itself a bright red. In ten years, physicians' fees have gone up 39 per cent and hospital costs 92 per cent. Weekly factory wages have risen 42 per cent, boosting lost-income settlements. Typical repair bills have climbed more than 50 per cent. As a result, the average bodily-injury claim is up 31 per cent, the average property-damage claim 46 per cent.

What such arithmetic means, say insurance men, is that from 1956 to 1966 the industry paid out $1.6 billion more in liability claims than it received in premiums. Critics answer that this "underwriting loss" actually stems from the unusual accounting used in seeking higher rates. For one thing, the companies put aside a large portion of their premiums as "unearned reserves," count them as a nontaxed liability—and then invest them along with other reserves. And when it comes to setting rates, critics add, the companies refuse to consider their investment profits. Still the industry's over-all profits are less than 6 per cent—just about the lowest of any major U.S. business. It is only by dipping into investment income that many auto insurers stay in the black.

Chief source of their trouble is the widely misunderstood liability coverage—which is quite unlike other forms of insurance. When a person buys fire, medical or collision insurance, his company pays him directly for his losses. But a liability policy does not protect a driver against the cost of injury to himself; it protects him against the possibility of having to pay for someone else's injuries in the event that a court finds him at fault. Once that happens, the driver's company must pay the judgment against him. And with its own money at stake, the company usually tries to beat down the victim's claims, however just. As damage awards mount, the industry compensates for its losses by raising everyone's premiums. But even when a company wins in court and does not have to pay a claim, it may still retaliate against its policyholder by canceling his insurance, a fate that makes other companies regard him as such a poor risk that he finds it very hard to buy a new policy.

Preferred Risks

Compounding this recipe for hostility between all parties is the difficulty of assessing the legal responsibility for auto accidents. In the six states (Arkansas, Maine, Mississippi, Nebraska, South Dakota, Wisconsin) that have "comparative negligence" laws, a victim who is partly responsible for a crash can recover a proportionate percentage of his losses. In the other forty-four states, unless the victim can prove that the policyholder was entirely at fault—and that he himself was utterly blameless—the company need not pay him a cent. Indeed, the worse the accident—a ten-car chain collision, for example—the more difficult it usually is to pin sole blame on one driver and reimburse anyone. If a driver has a heart attack and his car mounts a curb, hitting ten pedestrians, who is at fault? No one. Who gets paid? No one.

Almost inevitably, the fault system results in wildly erratic settlements. Insurance companies are notorious for overpaying small "nuisance" claims because it would cost more to fight them than to settle. At the same time, the seriously injured victim with high economic losses is often unable to wait for his case to come to trial and is forced to settle for whatever the company offers. If he does gamble on going to court, he may lose the case and get nothing. On the other hand, if he wins he may hit the jackpot.

So much money is involved that it seems to nourish corruption. There are adjusters who take bribes to settle cases, plaintiffs who file inflated claims, witnesses who remember the unrememberable, doctors who commit perjury, and lawyers who squander their talents working for contingent fees (30 per cent of what they win for their clients), which now provide roughly one third of the U.S. bar's total income.

So great is the cost of lawyers' fees and overhead that it takes an estimated $2.20 in premiums and taxes to get $1 to an accident victim. (Blue Cross delivers $1 in benefits for $1.07.) Nor is inefficiency the only drawback of the ponderous system. Although only 5 per cent of auto cases ever reach trial, they still preempt about 65 per cent of the nation's civil-court calendars. It now takes two and a half years to get a civil case tried in most cities.

The fault system also forces insurers to compete almost entirely for "preferred risks"— drivers who seldom drive and people most likely to impress juries if they do get into trouble. As a result, thousands of unpreferred motorists have been unceremoniously stripped

of their policies or forced to pay sky-high surcharges, not only because of accidents, but sometimes because they happen to live in
"red line" (claim-prone) areas or belong to supposedly risky
groups—a category that includes the young, the old, Negroes,
actors, barbers, bartenders, sailors, soldiers and men with frivolous
nicknames like "Shorty." Divorcees are often blackballed because
they might irk women jurors; doctors and clergymen are frowned
upon as "preoccupied" drivers. A Manhattan lawyer was banned
after someone hit his car in his apartment-house parking lot
while he was upstairs asleep; a California housewife with a perfect
driving record lost her policy because her husband was a Navy
medic—driving an ambulance in Vietnam.

All states have "assigned-risk" plans, requiring every insurance
company to accept a quota of castoffs, whom they sometimes charge
150 per cent above standard rates for minimum coverage. For some
accident-prone drivers, even that price may be a bargain, but insurance companies have been so fast and loose about canceling
policies that many of those dumped into the assigned-risk pool do
not deserve it. In 1964-1965, for example, almost 70 per cent of
New York's assigned-risk drivers had clean driving records.

Painless Finance

Problems have proliferated so rapidly that soon only the Government may be able to handle the financial hazards of auto insurance. But how? In 1869, the Supreme Court ruled that "insurance
is not commerce," thus exempting it from Federal antitrust laws
and congressional regulation of interstate commerce. In 1945, after
the court had reversed itself, the McCarran-Ferguson Act put all
insurance under state supervision. But many congressmen now believe that the states are flunking the auto-insurance part of their
job. A Senate subcommittee has called for a "root and branch"
investigation of the entire industry. President Johnson echoed the
request in his State of the Union message last week, and Senate
hearings are due this spring. One likely result is that the McCarran-Ferguson Act may be amended to impose Federal standards on
lax state insurance commissions.

As if to ward off that result, more state commissions are holding public rate hearings, denying premium boosts and ordering insurers to specify their reasons for cancellations and nonrenewals. But none of this will lower the price of insurance. As cancellations decrease, the industry will find itself handling more high-risk drivers and paying out more in damages. To reduce their losses, they will be forced to raise premiums still higher.

Somehow the industry must be helped to cut its costs. One obvious step is tighter state driver-licensing—or even a Federal license for all U.S. drivers. If 20 per cent of the country's drivers lost their licenses, says the Stanford Research Institute, the accident rate would go down 80 per cent.

Some critics urge the Federal Government to do the insurance industry a favor and take over the auto-accident business entirely. Urban specialist Daniel P. Moynihan, who chairs a Federal auto-safety advisory committee, suggests a Federal insurance system modeled on workmen's compensation, with awards made strictly on the basis of loss rather than fault. "Financing such a system," he argues, "might be the easiest part of all." Some $3.4 billion a year in gasoline taxes is already being spent to build the Interstate Highway System. When the system is finished in 1973, Moynihan would simply raise the gas tax a penny or so a gallon and switch the revenue to insurance, for which motorists would pay no other premium.

There are serious objections to Moynihan's nonfault Government insurance scheme, however tidy it sounds. For one thing, it would be fought hard by the oil industry, which aches to repeal the present gas tax. For another, it might be so financially painless that U.S. drivers would tend to worry less about their liability for accidents. And Government insurance might become a political football as legislators vied to curb needed rate raises.

Most experts still feel that private enterprise, with all its built-in advantages of business competition, should be given a second chance rather than a death sentence. They argue that the way to cut auto-insurance costs is to design a system that automatically compensates most victims regardless of fault, and still gives them the option of going to court to ask for more. Such mixed systems are already operating in several other countries, notably in Canada's Saskatchewan Province, where auto insurance costs two thirds as much as identical coverage in adjoining North Dakota.

A much discussed mixed system geared to the United States is now being advocated by Law Professors Robert E. Keeton of Harvard and Jeffrey O'Connell of the University of Illinois. [See the following article.—Ed.] In their book *After Cars Crash*, they propose a novel form of auto insurance called "Basic Protection," which would pay benefits more widely and efficiently, yet preserve both private enterprise and the right to file lawsuits for severe injury and economic loss.

Under BP, all motorists would carry compulsory insurance that started paying victims immediately, regardless of who was at fault. The injured motorist, his passengers and any pedestrians he hit would be paid directly by his own insurance company—not the other fellow's—up to $10,000 per person and $100,000 per accident, mainly for medical expenses and wage losses up to $750 a month. Collateral benefits from Blue Cross and other sources, which juries are not permitted to consider when setting awards, would be deducted from BP payments; but such collateral coverage would entitle motorists to lower premiums. BP would also exclude property damage and payment for pain and suffering, which the authors consider a boondoggle in most cases. Even so, motorists could insure themselves and their families at extra cost against pain, inconvenience and "catastrophe" losses above $100,000.

Out of Business

If a victim's losses exceeded BP limits, he could still go to court and sue for damages above $10,000, plus pain and suffering if it amounted to more than $5,000. In turn, a BP-insured motorist would be personally liable for paying judgments exceeding those amounts.

Some experts claim that BP would cut insurance costs as much as 25 per cent, while compensating 25 per cent more victims. A few top companies favor parts of the plan; Insurance Company of North America has run newspaper ads supporting it. Pessimistic insurance men, however, foresee costlier, slower claim procedures, rising payments to now uncompensated victims—and no letup in accident suits because claims above BP would still attract swarms of contingent-fee lawyers. The American Trial Lawyers Association (the negligence bar) does not agree. It seems to fear that BP would put them out of business. In fact, after the scheme won the support of 250 Boston lawyers last summer and unexpectedly swept past the lower house of the Massachusetts legislature, a lobby of panicked negligence lawyers killed it in the state senate. The plan is pending or soon to be introduced in the legislatures of California, Connecticut, Illinois, Minnesota, New Jersey, Rhode Island and Wisconsin—in all of which negligence lawyers are fighting it.

Whatever the outcome, debate over the Keeton-O'Connell plan ought to spur auto insurers to self-reform. Some big companies have already moved toward nonfault by using an "advance payments" plan: if their policyholder is clearly liable, the victim is immediately paid for his out-of-pocket losses—without being asked to waive his right to any future settlement. The companies report that such claimants seldom sue later on. Other companies, notably State Farm Mutual and Allstate, have cut overhead by using computerized billing and their own low-commission salesmen rather than outside agents. Auto insurers might also save the public millions by selling group policies to companies and unions. Beyond that, they could swing their weight behind safer car design. If auto insurers offered big discounts for cars with easily repaired fenders or sturdy bumpers of uniform height, Detroit might soon find that it would pay to provide them.

The trouble is that many of these ideas are still just that—ideas. With bright exceptions, too many auto insurers refuse to believe that sweeping reform is needed, that exasperated motorists across the land are awakening to the suggestion that far better coverage is possible.

Two courses are open. One is Government auto insurance, which the industry dreads as a door-opener to further Government intervention in the insurance business. The other is fast industry action proving that private enterprise can best serve the motoring public. In every state legislature, the industry can and should unite to pit its great lobbying power against the negligence lawyers and in favor of a nonfault system—the Keeton-O'Connell plan, perhaps, or an even better one, if insurance experts can devise it.

A NEW PLAN FOR CAR INSURANCE [5]

Already Congress is . . . [investigating] some of the grosser and more obvious evils of automobile insurance. What are the problems of the present system, and what kind of changes should be made?

Professor Robert Keeton of the Harvard Law School and I propose a plan which we call the "Basic Protection Plan" under which the bulk of automobile insurance claims would be paid as fire insurance claims are paid—by one's own insurance company, for out-of-pocket loss and without regard to anyone's fault. Just as your fire insurance company pays for the loss you suffer when your house burns, regardless of whether you were careless with a lighted cigarette, so, under the Basic Protection Plan, your automobile insurance company would pay you for out-of-pocket loss, regardless of negligence. (But just as fire insurance doesn't cover intentionally burning your house, so one who intentionally injures himself in a traffic accident would not be paid by Basic Protection insurance.)

Basic Protection is an extension of the idea of the medical payments coverage one can buy in an automobile insurance policy today. A person injured in an automobile accident would be reimbursed for doctor bills, hospital bills, and the like, and also for lost wages. The insurance company would be required to pay month by month, as losses occurred, rather than delaying till the injured person and the company could agree on a lump sum settlement.

The second main feature of the plan is that a new law would do away with claims based on negligence unless the damages were higher than $5,000 for pain and suffering or $10,000 for all other items such as medical expense and wage loss. This would mean that all but a very small percentage of the claims for personal in-

[5] From *Crises in Car Insurance—Cause and Cure*, remarks by Jeffrey O'Connell at AMA briefing "Modernizing Insurance Marketing Plans," August 24, 1967, New York City. American Management Association. Press Relations Dept. 135 W. 50th St. New York 10020. '67. mimeo. Reprinted by permission. Mr. O'Connell is professor of law at the University of Illinois, College of Law, Champaign, Ill.

juries in automobile accidents would be handled entirely under the new Basic Protection coverage. The wasteful expense of bickering over fault—with all the cost of the time of investigators, lawyers, and courts—would be eliminated in all but the small percentage of cases in which injuries were severe.

As originally drafted, the Basic Protection Plan did not cover property damage. Recently, however, Professor Keeton and I have drafted a change under which a motorist can choose to include damage to his own car under his Basic Protection coverage, or, in the alternative, retain his present liability coverage for the property damage he causes to others. In the latter case, he would also probably want to carry collision insurance covering damage to his own car. By calling for only one coverage instead of two, the Basic Protection insurance applicable to property damage would be more efficient and cheaper.

One result of putting this new system into effect would be to cut sharply the overhead of the present system, which delivers so much less than 50 cents of the premium dollar to the pockets of victims. Of course this greater efficiency would help to reduce insurance costs. Also, doing away with lump sum awards and damages for pain and suffering in the multitude of small cases would remove the chief opportunities for fraud in the present system.

Problems of the Present System

The fundamental difficulty with present automobile insurance is that you can be paid after a traffic accident only by making a claim (1) against the other driver's insurance company, (2) on the basis that such other driver was at fault in causing the accident and that you were blameless, and (3) for a completely uncertain amount that includes not only out-of-pocket loss but payment for pain and suffering—whatever that is "worth" in money. The result is that all traffic claims today are dominated by attitudes of distrust and even outright hostility accompanying any negligence lawsuit.

The present system not only clogs our courts but is highly wasteful and expensive. Studies show that $2.20 must be paid in for each dollar that is paid out to an injured accident victim. The system leaves many victims either totally uncompensated or with only a fraction of their loss paid. On the other hand, the present system provides generous and even profligate compensation to others—especially among the trivially injured.

Suppose that instead of proposing to apply a system like fire insurance to automobile insurance, I were to suggest the opposite—namely applying the auto insurance system to fire insurance? After a fire, a victim could be paid for his loss:

1. Only if he could prove that someone else was at fault or that he was free from fault (e.g., if he had failed to reshingle his roof with fire resistant materials, he couldn't recover, with all the attendant problems of proof).

2. Only after he had hired a lawyer to press a claim against someone else's insurance company which felt no loyalty toward him

3. Only after months or—more likely—years of delay

4. Only after squabbling over a totally indeterminate amount (for example, assume after a fire a homeowner would be entitled to claim not only for his out-of-pocket loss, such as the market value of his burned couch, but also for his pain and suffering arising from the fact that his beloved Aunt Minnie gave him the couch, with all the attendant problems of proof here, too).

No one would ever agree to trade the present fire insurance system for the jungle I have just outlined. And yet, in essence, is [this] not just what those who propose to retain the present system are suggesting for auto insurance?

Isn't it time we paid the traffic accident victim like the victim of a fire—promptly, graciously and fairly, and without having to pay a third of what he is paid to a lawyer?

By doing so under the Basic Protection plan, not only would substantially more motorists be paid and paid promptly, but automobile insurance premiums would be *substantially* reduced. An independent study by Frank Harwayne of New York City, one of the nation's most eminent casualty actuaries, estimates *conservatively* that if the Basic Protection plan were enacted in New York State, 25 per cent more auto victims would be paid at about 25 per cent less cost.

X-RAYS AND TV SETS [6]

In October 1966, Dr. John N. Ott reported that rats placed near a color TV receiver became very lethargic. Dr. Ott concluded from his experiments that the picture tube in a TV set was a weak source of X-rays and that viewers would be be wise to keep more than four feet away from the screen when watching TV. His findings were considered sufficiently important to be reported to a special White House Committee on the effects of radiation, to the American Society of Motion Picture and Television Engineers, to several medical conventions and to the United States Public Health Service. (In this connection Consumers' Research, Inc. [publishers of *Consumer Bulletin*] as long ago as 1952 and in ensuing years, had mentioned the potential hazard, particularly to children, who often tend to sit close to or play around a set while it is operating.)

In May 1967 the General Electric Company announced that 90,000 color receivers of their manufacture might be expected to exhibit an X-radiation level that was above the accepted maximum safe level. The company at that time desired wide publicity for their announcement because they wished to modify the sets immediately and at their expense so as to eliminate the hazard which they had first discovered in November 1966.

The needed modifications were to be made by the GE distributor-dealer organizations, making use of factory-distributor-dealer records covering sales, warranty, financing, and service records. The company indicated then that the radiation went directly downward into the area beneath the set and that the program would be completed by July 1.

In the following week Congressman Paul Rogers of Florida requested on the floor of Congress that public hearings be scheduled to investigate the problem of the possibility of radiation to television viewers. At the same time, Underwriters' Laboratories announced their intention to reduce their accepted limit of 2.5 mr. (milliroentgens) per hour for X-radiation from a TV receiver to 0.5 mr. per hour. They further proposed that the effective date for this change be moved back from March 1969 to September 1967.

[6] From "X-ray Hazard in TV Sets." *Consumer Bulletin.* 50:4+. O. '67. Reprinted by permission of Consumer Bulletin, Washington, N.J. 07882. Copyright 1967.

In the weeks and months following the original announcement there was much discussion in the news media regarding GE's problem and the dangers of excessive radiation in general. It was revealed that the General Electric color sets in question were table and console models with 18-inch or larger picture tubes which had been produced between June 1966 and February 1967.

Later sources indicated the defect was present in sets sold between September 1966 and June 1967. More specifically, the tubes involved were specified as 6EF4's and 6LC6's (not the picture tubes, as some suspected), and the set serial numbers were given as starting with the letters OA or OD (though some carried no serial number identification).

As late as July 24 [1967], there were indications that 8 per cent of the 112,000 sets that were distributed (over 150,000 had been produced) were still to be found and modified by GE. On August 15, it was said that 1,877 were still to be found and corrected. By that time, too, various announcements in the press had indicated that the hazard involved in the emission of X-rays from color television sets varied from "negligible" to definite serious dangers to health.

The very confused picture that is presented to the technically uninformed consumer regarding the potential danger from radiation is probably brought about because no one knows just where the maximum exposure level should be set, for safety. In 1950, H. J. Muller, a Nobel-prize-winning geneticist, indicated that each 10 roentgens of radiation per year, applied every year, will have the effect, on the average, of shortening the life span of the individual by one year. The *Recommendations of the International Commission on Radiological Protection and of the International Commission on Radiological Units*, an NBS [National Bureau of Standards] Handbook published in mid-1951, allowed 0.5 roentgen in any one week for whole body exposure and 1.5 roentgens per week for partial exposure of the hands and forearms "at the basal layer of the epidermis."

Since the latter exposure condition would more closely approximate the potential danger from a GE receiver, it is interesting to note that, by comparison, if one assumes 3 hours of viewing TV each day, the present allowable levels for X-radiation and those recommended by the National Council on Radiation Protection and Measurement and by others in 1960 are only about 1/150 of those considered safe in 1950.

The nature of the hazard connected with high energy radiation may not be clearly understood by the average person. Actually, radiation causes injury to a person by damaging or killing many of the tiny living cells of which our bodies are composed so that the cells cannot do their normal work in the body. When radiation strikes a cell, whether in the skin or within the body, it disturbs its electrical balance and causes it to break up, or suffer some subtle modification. There may be other effects as well.

Actually, cells are always dying and being replaced as a part of the natural process of living. It is only when the rate of cell destruction is excessive over a long period of time or when excess exposure to radiation damages or destroys too many cells at one time that sickness or death may result.

There is also good evidence that exposure to any account of high energy radiation, no matter how small, may produce irreversible mutations (alterations of inheritable characteristics). The damage done is thought to be cumulative and would not be related to a certain minimum or threshold level, as is the case with immediate X-ray damage (which may or may not be detectable by ordinary means available to physicians). A dose causing a mutation might not produce a visible effect for years; the harm may be great, yet not evident till the next or succeeding generations.

In general terms, an amount of radiation that causes any detectable damage or injury can be considered to be overexposure. The permitted limits of exposure, however, vary, depending upon the nature of the exposure and its time relationship. In treating cancer, for example, a physician might expose a patient to an amount of radiation which might be reasonably safe on widely separated occasions but would be dangerous if applied on a daily basis. Indeed, the physician might "overexpose" to the extent that his patient is "burned" or becomes ill, but this is planned overexposure to do what is possible in combating the disease.

It is likely, because of the downward direction of the radiation, that no one has been seriously harmed by one of the defective GE color receivers. The potential hazard was likely greater with young children, who frequently tend to view programs from a position on the floor, or very close to the set.

The one good thing that has happened as a result of the GE color TV incident is that Congress has been alerted. Very possibly this will result in state and Federal legislation that will help protect the consumer from possible future design errors and quality-control deficiencies of the kind we have discussed.

SOMETHING FISHY [7]

Now that the legislators have tightened up on meat inspection because of unsanitary conditions in some packing plants, they'll be turning to similar problems in seafood. The result is likely to be a law calling for, among other things, regular Federal inspection of the output of fish processing plants; present inspection is very limited.

Though Congress and the Administration have long held back, prospects for such a measure suddenly seem to be picking up. Consumer advocate Ralph Nader, who has lobbied quietly but effectively on a number of issues, has begun pushing for a fish inspection law. And word is circulating that President Johnson is preparing to send Congress a tough proposal. . . .

The Government, say advocates of legislation, should do more to prevent outbreaks of disease that result from eating contaminated fish. Nine people died in 1963 from botulism poisoning after eating canned tuna, they recall, and during one weekend in 1966 nearly 400 cases of salmonella poisoning were reported in New York City; they were traced to fish from unsanitary plants.

An Alarming Report

A Food and Drug Administration inspection report on one plant tells this horror story:

Employees handled dirty burlap bags, then handled the fish. . . . The manager of the night shift wiped his hands on a rag in his pocket,

[7] From "With a Prod by Nader. U.S. Mulls a Clean-Up of Fish Processors," by Fred L. Zimmerman, staff reporter. *Wall Street Journal.* p 1+. Ja. 12, '68. Reprinted by permission.

then returned to . . . packing the fish. . . . The fish were allowed to stand at room temperature for approximately four and a half hours before they were placed in a refrigerator. . . . Fish dropped on the floor were picked up and returned to the table. . . . Fish were stored near open containers of garbage. The firm maintained an all-purpose barrel of warm water which was used to rinse off fish which had dropped to the floor, to clean barrels and workers' hands, and later to rinse the fish off before they were hung.

Another consideration facing Congress is simply the tastiness of seafood. Many authorities believe it would be improved if the Government sought to assure the wholesomeness of the fish supply by requiring prompt processing and proper refrigeration. They add that if quality were higher, sales would be, too.

"Frankly, the segments of the industry that I have been familiar with need cleaning up very, very badly," Lowell Wakefield, president of Wakefield Fisheries at Port Wakefield, Alaska, told a Senate Commerce subcommittee last summer. "The fishy stench that is characteristic of seafoods in the minds of so many customers just should not exist at all."

Mr. Wakefield, a forty-six-year veteran of the fishing industry, said smelly fish result from "low quality standards" and that "this situation costs our industry countless millions of dollars in lost sales."

A "Penance Food"

Despite the wide availability of frozen fish, annual per-capita consumption of seafood in this country has held at an average of only 10 or 11 pounds for more than a generation. Consumers Union, a nonprofit testing organization that regularly surveys fish quality, asserts that "most people seldom get to taste the sweet, delicate flavor of fresh-caught fish. . . . By the time it reaches the dinner table, it has usually attained an age and condition warranting its religious connotation as a penance food."

A desire to bolster lagging sales is a key reason Democratic Senator Philip Hart of Michigan introduced a bill more than a year ago that provides for Federal sanitation standards covering processing plants and fishing vessels. "Senator Hart wants to sell more fish" from the Great Lakes region, says a participant in last year's hearings on the Hart bill. Even so, the legislation has not gone

anywhere, mainly because of the Johnson Administration's past opposition. This opposition sprang partly, it's said, out of reluctance
to see a potentially expensive new program started at a time of
budget strains.

But passage of the tough meat inspection law has spurred interest in the fish bill as a logical sequel. And Mr. Nader is applying
pressure. As usual, he's working mostly behind the scenes, but he
surfaced briefly . . . with a *New Republic* article designed to aid
the cause.

He criticized much of the U.S. fishing fleet as "old and grossly
unsanitary." He said too much time passes between catching and
processing of fish and charged that fish often are stored at tempera-
tures high enough to "bring deteriorating havoc on this highly
perishable commodity." Mr. Nader also complained about "sloppy
processing practices" that he said were dangerous to health. He
called for strong legislation to solve all these problems.

The Hart bill, which Mr. Nader terms "eminently weak,"
would have the Secretary of the Interior first make a survey of the
fishing industry. Then, three years after the bill's passage, he
would issue "adequate sanitary standards" for processing plants
and fishing vessels, but they wouldn't take effect for another three
years. Vessels under five tons would be exempted, as would wholesale fish markets.

Unlike the Hart proposal, Mr. Johnson's plan will probably provide for Federal inspection of processing plants, perhaps on a continuous basis by a "resident" inspector. Further, the Administration
will probably want to shrink Senator Hart's proposed six-year gap
between passage of the bill and the time its inspection provisions
take effect. [President Johnson requested legislation on February
6, 1968. Hearings on the Administration bill began in April.—Ed.]

Even this tougher plan might be generally acceptable to much
of the seafood industry, judging by testimony its envoys gave at the
Senate hearings last summer. But industry men are sure to bring up
two complicating issues, and it's unclear how Congress will resolve
them.

One of these complications is the question of inspecting imported
fish, which constitute about half the total volume of seafood con-

sumed in the United States. The other is the question of whether the
law should call for inspection of the thousands of American fishing
vessels; that would add substantially to the cost of an inspection
program.

CONSUMERS AND COMPUTERS [8]

The age of the nonhero and the hippie freak-out has a new addition—the nonresponse of business, particularly in the retail industry.

The nonresponse has many variations. In its most elemental
form, it is a nonresponse to a letter of complaint. It is a nonresponse
that arrives weeks, sometimes months, after a letter is written, but
says little or nothing and is not acted upon....

Department stores, one of the principal offenders in the nonresponse, put the blame on computers. Undoubtedly, the complexities of automation have caused problems for many businesses, including many that should never have indulged in the luxury of de-
personalizing their establishments. But the letters of complaint are
not addressed to computers; perhaps if they were, they would be answered. The letters are addressed to people who are paid to do certain tasks, one of which involves the long-lost art of soothing dis-
satisfied customers. But they do not answer these letters and only
their secretaries answer their phones....

Blame Is Shifted

Perhaps the best way of demonstrating the dimensions of the
problem is with one specific case history of a nonresponse.

This one began on Sunday, May 7, 1967, when a newspaper advertisement attracted the eye of a woman customer. She greatly admired a dress and a pants suit advertised by a prestigious fashion-
conscious department store, and telephoned the next day to order one
of each.

When they arrived, they did not live up to her expectations. She
called again, explained that she rarely ordered things by phone, that
it had been a mistake, and please take them back. The articles were
picked up on Friday, May 12; she received a receipt.

[8] From "Customers Encounter Non-Response," by Lee Kanner assistant to financial
and business editor. New York *Times.* p 14F. N. 12, '67. © 1967 by The New York
Times Company. Reprinted by permission.

Time passes. The incident is forgotten. The monthly bill arrives, the $41.82 charge for the dress and pants suit is listed. It is ignored, with the optimistic expectation that the computer will catch up with the credit the following month. The rest of the bill is paid, however.

Another month, another bill. The $41.82 is still there, big as life. The customer picks up the phone, reaches someone in the credit office, explains the situation and is assured everything will be all right the next month.

The August bill adds a new dimension—the first irritating dunning notice. Infuriated, the husband writes a letter to the store, giving all the necessary details, including the receipt number for the articles returned. He requests that the matter be straightened out immediately so that his wife can again use the charge account.

Weeks later, on October 3, he received the following reply:

"Thank you for your recent letter. It has been referred to our bill adjustment manager, and I am sure you will hear from him shortly."

The letter, signed by the director of charge accounts, was obviously a nonresponse letter referring the matter to the proper department where it undoubtedly would be forgotten. It did not deceive the husband, but the wife was encouraged. More important, she needed a pair of shoes and a winter coat. The husband yielded, the wife went shopping in her favorite store. She bought the shoes, but no coat. She wanted her husband to help select it, and he agreed to return with her.

Two weeks passed before he could accompany her. By this time even he was hopeful that the charge account error had been cleared up. Anyway, the amount involved was so small he considered the matter more of an annoyance than anything else.

He liked two coats on his wife, a dress coat and a sport model, and, in a fit of reckless generosity, told her to buy both. Total cost $395.

Naturally, this entailed a check of his charge account by the delighted saleswoman. The customers waited, and waited, and waited. Finally, with many apologies, the saleswoman asked them to accompany her to the charge account office, where a colleague was attempting to convince the main office to release the coats.

With growing irritation, but still convinced that the delay was not serious, the husband explained to the credit worker why he had not paid the $41.82 and what he and his wife had been doing about it for months.

Nothing helped. The main office insisted the bill was overdue since May, and there was no record of any letters written or answered, or of any telephone calls. Since the husband did not have the store's letter with him, he could not even supply the name of the man who had written him.

No one doubted him, but no one could do anything. Again the computer was blamed, but this was not the fault of automation, it was a human error in noncommunication, the failure of people working in the same store, probably in the same office, to note on his account the fact that he had written and his wife had called several times.

The couple stamped out angrily, entered the store of a nearby competitor and purchased a dress coat. By the time they arrived back home, the telephone was ringing. It was the saleswoman in the first store. The sale had been cleared, should she send the coats? Mollified, the husband told her to send the sport coat, but that she had lost the sale of the more expensive coat because of the incompetence in the charge office. The saleswoman voiced regret and sympathy with him, assured him it would never happen again.

$41.82 Still There

A happy ending? Had the store finally redeemed itself after the loss of at least $300 or $400 in sales over the last few months? Of course not. The monthly bill arrived two weeks later with the $41.82 still starkly staring out.

The husband called Mr. Blank, who had written the letter to him. A secretary answered. Mr. Blank was out, what was the call about? Would Mr. Blank call him back, please? No, not unless he knew what it was about. It was about a bill. That was not Mr. Blank's department, unless merchandise was being held up. Nothing was being held up, not any more. Then call Mr. Cipher (to whom Mr. Blank had referred in his letter).

Mr. Cipher was reached on the phone. Or rather, his secretary. Is he in? No, Mr. Cipher is out to lunch. Please have him call. What is it about? A bill. Mr. Cipher never calls anyone back about bills. But this has been going on since May. That doesn't matter, we have complaints that are unsettled since last November. The computers require time to straighten a new system out. But Mr. Blank suggested I call Mr. Cipher. You'll just have to wait your turn.

"Cancel My Account"

A last explosion by the husband: "Cancel my account!"

End of charge account. End of case history.

Is there a solution to the nonresponse problem? The department stores say time and better training will overcome all difficulties. The facts say no. Computers have apparently eliminated so many office workers that those remaining cannot cope with the tide of paper work. The nonpersonalized numbers game of the computers inevitably will more and more dehumanize relations between retail establishments and their customers. Apparently, customers—or former customers—will all have to learn to live with this depressing fact of life.

V. THE CONSUMER INTEREST MOVEMENT

EDITOR'S INTRODUCTION

The consumer interest movement dates from the mid-nineteenth century if construed to include the cooperative societies organized on the principles laid down in 1844 by the Rochdale Society in England.

The contemporary consumer movement, little more than a generation old, is now undergoing something of a rebirth or marked growth with new vigor being displayed by such organizations as Consumers Union and the rise of consumer groups in many sectors of society. These on-going developments are discussed in this section by Sidney Margolius, a free-lance specialist on consumer affairs. An article from *Business Week* follows, reporting on Consumers Union; and then *Newsweek* gives an extensive run-down on Ralph Nader, who has successfully campaigned for greater consumer protection on several fronts such as auto safety and inspection of meat and fish.

In the last selection Stanley Dreyer, president of the Cooperative League of the U.S.A., deals with the cooperative movement today.

THE ON-GOING CONSUMER FIGHT [1]

A great deal of activity affecting consumers has taken place in the last three years, sometimes even a confusing amount. But the results in terms of consumer protection have been noticeably smaller.

Undoubtedly the nation's conscience has been aroused by exposures of the many ways moderate-income families are exploited as consumers—from the millions of garnishments levied on workers' pay checks each year to the blatantly-overpriced processed foods and medicines housewives are lured into buying.

[1] From "Consumer Rights: The Battle Continues," by Sidney Margolius, expert on consumer problems and columnist in the labor press. *American Federationist.* 74:1-4. Ap. '67. Reprinted by permission.

But the business backlash has been unusually sharp and surprisingly effective. The businessmen's campaign has reached a hysterical pitch that would be ludicrous if it had not proved so successful. Take, for example, Woodrow Wirsig, former editor of *Printers' Ink* and now president of the New York Better Business Bureau. Wirsig, one of the most inflammatory campaigners against consumer legislation, recently warned an advertising trade conference that the proconsumer efforts are really a conspiracy against business, calling these efforts: "A deep, radical and dangerous trend toward the separation of business from every other value in life. . . . If legislation proceeds as it is going, we will inevitably have *a controlled economy with a controlled society.*" (Emphasis his.)

More restrained in their language, but perhaps even more influential in their opposition to the efforts on behalf of consumers, have been the officials of several large food and soap corporations. The most notable have been W. B. Murphy, president of the Campbell Soup Company and until recently chairman of the Business Advisory Council, and Neil McElroy, a former Eisenhower cabinet member and now head of Procter and Gamble.

President Johnson has continued to support proposed legislation despite the business backlash and has continued the post of Consumer Assistant at the White House level. But the business opposition has been so stubborn that it has become difficult to win any significant legislation except when actual safety is involved. Thus, except for the partial truth-in-packaging law, the only recent major consumer legislation enacted at the Federal level have been the laws concerned with car safety, with protection against hazardous toys and with safety in other children's articles.

Advances Noted

There has been, however, a number of advances in consumer organization and protection.

One is the unusual number of consumer associations organized in the past two years and the noticeably greater consciousness of many citizens that they are consumers as well as wage earners and need to defend themselves on both flanks. There are now some sixteen state consumer associations and almost as many city-wide groups. Labor unions and individual labor officials have been noticeably active in helping to organize these associations, along with representatives of credit unions; consumer co-ops; church groups; the leading Negro organizations; women's groups such as the American Association of University Women and Catholic, Jewish and Negro women's councils; state and local attorneys general; university economists and other community and political leaders and groups.

Similarly, a number of the local "Housewives for Lower Prices" and other boycott groups that spontaneously picketed supermarkets during the food-price upsurge . . . [in the fall of 1966] have continued in existence.

The national Consumer Assembly held in Washington . . . [in 1966] already has been followed by a similar assembly in New York City, with others expected to follow in other localities. The national Assembly, sponsored by thirty-two organizations, including the AFL-CIO, and representing a total membership of 50 million Americans, was credited by one state consumer official with persuading Congress to pass at least the diluted packaging bill.

A new vigor also is noticeable in the two major Federal agencies concerned with consumer protection—the Food and Drug Administration and the Federal Trade Commission. Under a determined new administrator, Dr. James L. Goddard, the FDA ordered off the market a number of products considered not effective or of doubtful usefulness, including antibiotic throat lozenges and several time-release aspirin products and other analgesics. The FDA also initiated, for the first time, seizure actions under the prescription advertising provisions of the Kefauver-Harris Drug Act. Perhaps even more significantly, the FDA has warned drugmakers that it will not tolerate misleading or incomplete drug advertising at either the consumer or professional levels (to doctors). [Dr. Goddard resigned on May 21, 1968—Ed.]

Similarly, the FTC announced new tire advertising guidelines to end some of the long-standing deceptive selling in that field. And it proposed regulations to require credit sellers to tell the full cost of products in their ads, not merely the monthly payment.

Another significant FTC activity is its current exploration, along with the Antitrust Division of the United States Attorney General's office, of the potential monopoly effect on consumer prices of heavy advertising expenditures by a few dominant corporations.

The third major advance is that state, county and municipal officials have been stirred into seeking to provide more adequate consumer protection, both through legislation and through establishment of state and local consumer councils and consumer protection bureaus.

In some cases, these new bureaus are an expansion of the traditional weights and measures departments. Now some seven states have consumer agencies of either the council or bureau type, similar proposals are pending in other states and consumer bureaus have been established or proposed in Cook County, Illinois; Nassau County, New York; and other areas.

The progress in developing consumer representation at the state level has not been without setbacks. In California, as soon as he took office, Governor Ronald Reagan fired Helen Nelson, California's capable Consumer Counsel, chopped the office's budget almost in half and named a real estate man's wife to be Consumer Counsel, with an order to investigate the usefulness of the agency and whether it should continue.

The Needs at This Point

The main need at this point is for effective legislation at both Federal and state levels to discourage the current exploitation of working families as consumers. "Exploitation" is not too strong a word to describe the present consumer situation, from children manipulated by TV ads and teenagers by disc jockeys to parents manipulated into habitual installment buying at high charges for the financing and often for the merchandise.

The result is a massive waste of family money and a diversion of both family and national resources that helps to frustrate such goals as higher education, the rehabilitation of the cities, better housing and more adequate health care.

Despite the business opposition, the public's heightened consumer consciousness and the growing interest of Federal and state legislators provide an opportunity to eliminate some of the most prominent abuses. Even some of the more reasonable business leaders, largely as the result of Mrs. Esther Peterson's persuasive efforts during her years as the President's Consumer Assistant, recently have told their fellow businessmen that some consumer protection may be necessary. Fair rules for the treatment of consumers would, of course, benefit the more scrupulous business organizations as well as the nation. . . .

[There is need for consumer education. But] seeking to solve current consumer problems primarily through "consumer education, which some business officials have proposed as an alternative to legislation, is like trying to swim in a sea of molasses.

For one reason, the families most susceptible to exploitation are the low- and moderate-income wage earners, and those only a generation away from the noncash world of the farm or the simpler, if deprived, money world of the poor. These people are the hardest to reach with consumer education.

For another reason, family money problems have become too complex to be solved simply with information. A family would need to become expert in shopping, nutrition, interest rates, mortgages and many other facts of today's complicated consumer world.

Urgent Needs Today

Truth-in-packaging. The law finally passed by Congress turned out to be more a "clear labeling" law than the law originally proposed by Senator Philip Hart (Democrat, Michigan). The original Hart bill would have eliminated the fractional ounces and other chaotic packaging practices now making it difficult to compare values. It now will be easier for shoppers to locate the statement of net contents on package labels. But you still have to try to compare the cost per ounce of, for example, different brands of tuna fish containing $5\frac{3}{4}$, $6\frac{1}{2}$, and $7\frac{1}{4}$ ounces.

The new packaging law does establish a significant principle. The preamble says the nation's economy depends on informed choice. For the first time, Congress has said that how the consumer spends his money, or is led to spend it, affects the nation's welfare.

Service and guarantee problems. This is an area Mrs. Peterson was exploring on a voluntary basis with industry spokesmen before she returned to full-time duty as an Assistant Secretary of Labor. Senator [Warren] Magnuson [Democrat, Washington] has entered this difficult but necessary area of consumer protection in two ways. His consumer subcommittee, established in the closing days of the Eighty-ninth Congress . . . , is investigating hazardous appliances and other household equipment. Senators Magnuson and Norris Cotton (Republican, New Hampshire) have proposed the establishment of a National Committee on Hazardous Household Products to study these dangers.

Senator Magnuson's committee also is investigating the costs and problems involved in guarantees and service on household appliances in general—a source of great irritation and tension in the marketplace.

Drug prices. Despite the Kefauver-Harris Drug Act, the problem of high prices of vital medicines still plagues consumers and now has become a problem in financing Medicare and other health plans. A number of senators and congressmen have become determined to encourage the use of generic drugs both for medicare-insured patients and the general public. Drugs under their generic names cost only a fraction of the same drugs under brand names.

Food prices. This remains one of the knottiest and also politically sensitive problems, for which neither the Administration nor Congress has proposed any far-reaching or over-all solutions. . . .

Consumer representation. The proposal by Representative Benjamin Rosenthal (Democrat, New York) to establish a Federal Department of Consumers has evoked discussion of the need for permanent consumer representation at the top levels of Government. Whether this representation should take the form of a full-fledged department or an independent consumer counsel office, it obviously is needed to defend the consumer interest on a permanent basis, making it less vulnerable to the attacks of soap kings and soup magnates.

Credit and installment plans. This is the area of most severe exploitation. It takes the form of deception leading often to garnishment and, surprisingly often, the loss of jobs and homes. And it is a constant drain on family income to pay needlessly high finance charges, even when financial tragedy does not result.

Both Federal and state laws are being sought. . . . When one observes that consumers now owe a total of $95 billion in debts, of which $75 billion is for installment credit, and pay finance charges of $13 billion a year on these debts, the paramount importance of . . . [such legislation] becomes clear.

On the state and provincial level, Massachusetts, Saskatchewan and Nova Scotia already have enacted their own truth-in-lending laws. In Massachusetts, however, stores are not required to tell the true annual rate on their revolving-credit or "budget charge" accounts—a serious loophole since stores can merely switch to this type of credit from the more-traditional installment plans.

Senator Warren Magnuson (Democrat, Washington) also has proposed a Fair Credit Advertising Act, which would require that credit ads tell the total credit cost instead of merely the weekly or monthly payments required, as well as the true annual interest.

But labor and other consumer-interest organizations also are increasingly concerned about the need for changes in present state laws governing installment practices. These stem from the days credit was not as widely used and they protect mainly the seller.

These laws have become widely abused to exploit unknowing buyers. The present garnishee and repossession laws actually serve as twin levers of financial coercion. In most states, credit sellers can both garnishee and repossess. Thus, fantastically enough, sellers can repossess installment goods and still compel the buyer to keep on paying even after he no longer has his goods. Many garnishees today are of that very nature—garnishees for deficiency judgments on repossessed purchases. The present effort at state levels is to change present laws to let sellers garnishee or repossess, but not both.

Even the threat of a garnishee often is enough to compel a workingman to pay for a deceptively-sold purchase because he fears the loss of his job. Notoriously, too, states which have harsh garnishee laws allowing creditors to seize a large part of the debtors' wages usually have most consumer bankruptcies. California, which permits garnishment of up to 50 per cent of wages, has a bankruptcy rate five times that of New York, which permits only 10 per cent.

In a half dozen states, unions are seeking laws to bar firings because of garnishment. In New Jersey, for example, such a bill has been introduced year after year without enactment. In Ohio, too, unions have been seeking similar relief for years. In New York, in 1966, unions broke through the legislative barricade of the credit-industry lobby to win passage of the first such law—a modified version which bars employers from firing because of one garnishee in a twelve-month period.

Other tools of deception presently written into the law in various states, which require correction, include the "cognovit" or "confession of judgment" installment contracts permitted in some states by which a buyer signs away his right to any court defense, and the "add-on" installment contracts permitted in most states. These make previous purchases security for new purchases, even though older purchases may be paid up.

THE ROLE OF CONSUMERS UNION [2]

To the 1.25 million people who buy *Consumer Reports*, the monthly magazine is nothing if not outspoken. For thirty-one years, it has been damning and praising thousands of new products, hypoing sales of some products, torpedoing others. In the process it has done its share to boost product quality, and made its publisher, Consumers Union of U.S., Inc., the center of countless controversies. . . .

Neither the controversy nor the reaction by industry is new for CU. But the speed of CU's impact on Federal regulatory agencies—coming at a time when interest in consumer protection is at an all-time high—portends a more active role for CU.

To be sure, CU's main weapon will still be information aimed at a manufacturer it rates as negligent or at a Government agency that it deems in need of a push. To broaden the impact of its in-

[2] From "Consumers Union Puts on Muscle." *Business Week.* p 84-6. D. 23, '67. Reprinted from the December 23, 1967, issue of *Business Week* by special permission. Copyright © 1967 by McGraw-Hill, Inc.

formation, CU expects to increase the circulation of *Consumer Reports* from the present 1.25 million to 2.5 million—5 per cent of all U.S. families—within five years. Two years ago sales of the magazine had leveled off at around 950,000 per month. CU then boosted circulation by one third to the current level. Promotion costs last year topped $1.7 million, 29 per cent of CU's budget of $6 million.

Suing Veterans Administration

Beyond the traditional role played by *Consumer Reports*, however, CU is finding new ways to have its voice echo in Washington's corridors of power—even though as a nonprofit, tax-exempt group it does not lobby directly. CU is planning to sue the Veterans Administration if VA doesn't release the results of its tests on hearing aids. By making a test case of the VA under the recently passed Public Information Act, CU hopes to prod other Government agencies. such as the Bureau of Standards, the General Services Administration, and the Defense Department, to release product information gathered with public funds.

CU also plans to set up a Washington office to gather and disseminate product information.

Adding to CU's action look is its newest board member: Ralph Nader. On his own, of course, Nader has dramatically and effectively championed the cause of safety in autos, meat packing, and gas pipelines. Working together, Nader and CU may both be still more effective in consumer causes. . . . The board voted to establish an annual "CU fellowship"—for a young lawyer to be put on its payroll. Though the details are not final, the first "fellow" will probably help in Nader's drive for strict safety standards for autos.

Warranties

Partly because of Nader's impact, the movement for greater consumer protection—sometimes called "consumerism"—has picked up steam in the last couple of years. Manufacturers have extended warranties on a wide variety of products, and are finding new ways to improve quality. Product liability suits have proliferated. Callbacks are no longer limited to the auto industry. Congress, often apathetic about consumer needs, has passed a spate of legislation— from auto safety to truth-in-packaging.

"The time is ripe" for CU to play a more active role, says President Colston Warne, an economics professor at Amherst College, who has headed CU since it was founded in 1936.

Although consumerism has eased the task somewhat, it has created new problems. With the Government now setting standards in a variety of industries, CU feels it has to keep one eye on manufacturers, the other on the Government. Our goal, says Executive Director Walker Sandbach, is not only to get new consumer legislation, but to see that the standards it sets are both strong and strongly enforced. Otherwise, he says, "we'd get a no-bill bill, or a no-law law."

Third Force

Sandbach, who joined CU two and a half years ago after heading Chicago's largest consumer cooperative, says that "industry's considerable influence in Washington often leads to the Government's working hand-in-hand with industry. There's a need for a third force to represent the consumer, and we want to play an important part."

Sandbach's ideas are backed by some Washington observers who detect a spreading industry tactic in dealing with the Government. They point to auto and tire makers that, they say, publicly supported safety standards for their industries, then influenced the final form of the standards in quiet negotiation.

Because CU doesn't officially lobby, its effectiveness as a third force depends on how good a job it does in its testing, how widely it can disseminate its information, and how much impact its disclosures have.

The Validity of CU's Approach

These questions, in turn, raise most of the traditional questions about CU: Are its tests complete, fair, accurate, and relevant for today's consumer? How much impact does CU have on consumer buying plans, manufacturers' quality control, and regulatory agencies?

Test Sites. CU tests 2,000 models in seventy product categories every year. Auto tests are conducted at a racetrack in Lime Rock, Connecticut, while almost all other products are tested at headquarters, a sixty-year-old converted factory in Mount Vernon, New York. With refrigerators, washers, vacuum cleaners, skis, broilers, baby strollers, and mattresses scattered about, the five laboratories look like the warehouse of a large department store before inventory.

CU shoppers buy the products at retail prices in stores around the country, without ever revealing that they will be tested. Some tests are rather standard. Others are devised by CU's staff of forty engineers, often using Rube Goldberg-like rigs. Recently, children's sneakers were tested by letting hundreds of youngsters wear them during their normal activities. And CU called a panel of students from the Juilliard School of Music to evaluate hi-fi tone quality after the equipment had been put through tests for frequency response, distortion, and other technical factors. If a defect shows up that CU considers to be serious—such as the gasoline spillage from the Ambassador sedan—it will test a second model.

Equipment. CU's labs, including textiles, electronics, and chemicals, are well equipped. It's white-robed engineers generate their own closed circuit TV signal for testing, use a "Faraday cage" to keep out unwanted interference in broadcast equipment tests, and recently added an "anechoic" (nonecho) chamber to test hearing aids.

When the staff is satisfied it has given each product a fair shake, the results are summarized in *Consumer Reports* as "acceptable" or "not acceptable." Often products are "check rated," which means outstanding quality, or labeled "best buy," which means outstanding quality for the price. Specifications of the product and test criteria are usually indicated, so the reader can decide if CU's reasons apply to him.

CU's readers are so far above average in salary and education that they are an ad manager's dream. But CU would no more accept advertising than Ralph Nader would work as a PR man for General Motors. Nor does CU allow manufacturers to use a favorable rating to promote one of its products. CU's reason: If its reputation for honesty is ever seriously questioned, its whole reason for being would crumble.

Hostile View

Though CU's honesty is rarely attacked, plenty of other criticisms—from charges of communism to prejudice against big business—have been hurled at CU over the years. The three most frequent accusations are inadequate test methods, too few samples and irrelevant criteria.

Says Dr. G. P. Daiger, engineering vice president of Hoover Company: "It's pretty impractical to think groups of this size can make conclusive tests. We don't question their integrity, but we do question their thoroughness." One TV manufacturer says if a single product is "accidentally not up to snuff, your name is mud." Another likens CU tests to "Russian roulette." John Crichton, president of the American Association of Advertising Agencies, faults CU for erratic and irrelevant interpretation of its tests. "Their reasons for downgrading a product are sometimes trivial or plain silly."

For all the criticism, CU has had a definite impact on sales and product quality, many manufacturers believe. Westinghouse credits a favorable rating for a 20 per cent jump in washing machines sales last year. Several years ago a Norge executive said flatly: "CU put us in the washing machine business."

Hi-fi Sales

In the "buff industries" such as hi-fis and cameras, sales impact is particularly strong. A San Francisco hi-fi component dealer says 5 per cent or 10 per cent of his customers arrive with an opinion influenced by *Consumer Reports*. And a hi-fi manufacturer says many customers write on their warranty cards that they first heard about the company's products through CU.

Countless manufacturers have improved their products because of a CU rating. Some examples: Clevite eliminated a shock hazard in a stereo headphone. Remington corrected a tendency for its electric knife to jam, and Westinghouse improved the design of its electric broiler. "Smart manufacturers," says Dr. Robert Entenberg, professor of marketing at the University of Denver, "use *Consumer Reports* to see if they can improve their products."

What consumer issues will be important in the next few years? Sandbach cites service problems—particularly auto and appliance repairs—auto and life insurance reforms, utility rates, and medical costs and quality. "You never know," he adds, "what issue will have the political sex appeal of auto safety or meat packing."

A ONE-MAN CRUSADE [3]

At thirty-three, working alone and armed only with his own zeal, a searching mind, inexhaustible energy and very little money, Ralph Nader has become the mainspring of a consumers' movement practically dormant since Upton Sinclair gored the packers of diseased and filthy meat with his book *The Jungle* back in 1906. If he is not yet king, the consumer is at least assured of a careful hearing on Capitol Hill—often for no more lofty reason than that he votes. During the past two years, Congress has passed laws setting Federal standards on auto safety, flammable fabrics, clinical laboratories and meat packing. This year, at the very minimum, it will tackle such consumer concerns as truth-in-lending, pipeline safety and mail-order selling. . . .

Nader's role in firing all this Washington activity on behalf of the long-forgotten consumer began four years ago. As a young attorney fresh from Harvard Law School, he had handled a number of auto-accident damage suits in his native Connecticut. Not only was he appalled with the highway death toll but he was vastly disturbed because all too often, only the driver was blamed—with little or no effort to find out if the car might be at fault. One result: Nader wrote *Unsafe at Any Speed,* a meticulously documented (and, as it turned out, best-selling) report on safety defects in Detroit's cars, primarily some of GM's early Corvairs. In early 1966 Nader, still relatively unknown, traveled up to Capitol Hill to testify before Senator Abraham Ribicoff's [Democrat, Connecticut] auto-safety committee. With his ragged gray tweed overcoat, his tie askew and his long, bony hands shooting out from his rumpled

[3] From "Meet Ralph Nader." *Newsweek.* 71:65-7+. Ja. 22, '68. Copyright Newsweek, Inc. January 22, 1968. Reprinted by permission.

suit, he looked for all the world like one of dozens of wild-eyed inventors who besiege the committee with auto-safety ideas, many of them bearing a strong resemblance to something inspired by Rube Goldberg. But this guy was different, a committee staffer recalled. "Nader wasn't selling anything," he said. . . . "He was a congressional staffer's dream; he had the data—the names and phone numbers to substantiate everything."

Besides data, it developed that Nader had something else—a shadow in the person of Vincent Gillen, a New York private detective working for General Motors for a $6,700 fee to find out what Nader's angle might be in attacking the Corvair (and also, according to Gillen's instructions to his operatives, to pry into Nader's private life). When the gumshoe story broke, Ribicoff and Senator Robert Kennedy [Democrat, New York] among others, were outraged; GM president (now board chairman) James Roche, who hadn't known about Gillen's assignment and was equally appalled, publicly apologized—and Ralph Nader was suddenly on the front page to stay. (Nader subsequently filed a $26 million damage suit against GM, but it will probably be several years before it reaches trial stage.)

The upshot was the first law putting the Government in the business of setting safety standards for all cars sold in the United States, domestic or foreign. For its part, Detroit became more safety-conscious than ever before, and is now spending millions in the pursuit of safer cars. A year later, Detroit still has mixed feelings about Nader. "If GM hadn't beatified him, where would he be today?" shrugs one auto man. But another says: "I feel that Nader's contribution was not so much in the safety arena per se, but in the voice and flesh he gave to the auto-buying public. He was, and is, a tough customer to please, but he showed there are lots more like him in our showrooms."

After his confrontation with GM, Nader's public image was more like that of a knight in shining armor. To masses of Americans chronically addicted to rooting for the underdog, there was something irresistibly appealing in the sight of a slender, boyish, vulnerable figure standing up to a giant industry—a latter-day incarnation of a Jimmy Stewart hero in a Frank Capra movie.

Today it still strikes many as more than a little incongruous
that Nader can exist in an age when most successful public move-
ments are a product of money and manpower. But exist he does, and
nothing makes Nader himself chuckle more than the notion that
he is some kind of lofty idealist. He has ideals, but he speaks in
hard-headed terms of using whatever leverage he can find to achieve
his aims, or of modifying his aims if he can't get all he wants. "I
deal," he says, "in the art of the possible."

Nader's Future

The possibles for Nader have grown infinitely since he achieved
his sudden fame in auto safety. Critics complain that he is too
"emotional," too "vindictive." But his charges and denunciations
now command headlines at home and abroad, and a simple letter
of inquiry from Nader to a Federal agency or industrial firm gets
immediate attention. Not long ago he dispatched a letter to the
Department of Transportation (asking why reports on railroad accidents are kept secret); the agency appointed a special committee
to draft an answer.

More importantly, perhaps, Nader has become a valued arm of
such consumer-minded senators as Washington's Warren Magnuson [Democrat], Minnesota's Walter Mondale [Democrat] and
Wisconsin's Gaylord Nelson [Democrat]. And he has tailored his
strategy to suit the situation. While he was both a public symbol
and highly visible witness at the auto-safety hearings, Nader as
often as not has served as an investigator and behind-the-scenes
strategist on other issues. As he put it last week: "If I can stay on
the sidelines and get three senators to say something, that's better
than if I said it myself. I don't need any more enemies." As an investigator and propagandist, on the other hand, Nader can assault
an issue on all fronts—a technique best demonstrated by the passage
of last year's meat-inspection bill.

Meat Feat

"Most inspection bills had been going up and down Capitol Hill
for years with little hope of passage," Betty Furness, the President's

own adviser on consumer affairs, recalled. . . . "The expectation was that '67 was a year like all years; there would be no meat bill." But Nader went to work anyway. In early July he whipped out the first of two articles on the subject for the *New Republic*. It was titled "We're Back in the Jungle" and documented the fact that 25 per cent of the meat sold in the United States—enough for 50 million people—was not subject to Federal inspection. Then he hit real paydirt—an unpublicized Agriculture Department report on meat-packing plants beyond Federal jurisdiction. A few of its more grisly sections were cited by President Johnson . . . when he signed the meat-inspection bill: "A man was wrapping pork shoulders. He dropped one in the sawdust, picked it up, wiped it off with a dirty, sour rag. . . . Beef was being broken on an open dock by a dirt road, in 95-degree weather. There were flies on the meat. Drums of bones and meat scraps were covered with maggots."

Nader packed a series of letters with this kind of evidence, mailed them to an influential congressman and released them to the press. He also took off on a ten-city tour stretching from Boston to Los Angeles detailing the meat story in newspaper and television interviews. The result: an avalanche of mail on the desk of Betty Furness. "You wouldn't believe the letters," she said. "They were from meat inspectors themselves, their wives, ordinary consumers—everybody—demanding tough action."

Back in Washington, Nader was a constant witness before the House Agriculture Committee, which was considering the meat-inspection bill. From the witness chair, Nader bore down on a favorite theme—the misallocation of resources and talent in many segments of U.S. society. "If we can spend between $100 million and $200 million a year on beautifying highways," he said, "we should be able to appropriate $45 million a year to clean up the meat mess."

As it turned out, the House passed a weak bill—but Nader was far from finished. During Senate hearings, he had a hand in surfacing a story that Western meat packers were threatening to withhold campaign contributions from certain congressmen who voted for a tough bill. At the same time, Nader put the heat on the White House to demand a Senate bill with real teeth—a measure providing for the mandatory Federal inspection of all U.S. meat. Finally, Miss Furness took a stand, and bowing to this and grass-roots pressures the Senate eventually passed a tough bill (by a vote of 89-2) in late November [1967]. As one Senate source summed up Nader's performance: "The meat bill was Ralph's finest hour. He was calmer than when he first emerged on the auto-safety battle, more able to accept events. On meat, he realized that any victory was terrific." . . .

What Makes Nader Run?

Washington, a cynical city with more than its share of people on the make, still can't quite believe it is dedication alone. One story has it that he's salting away fat payoffs earned by referring accident cases to law firms (the seventy or so letters he gets every day from outraged citizens would give him ample opportunity to do so). On the Capital cocktail circuit, other chatter has it that his shabby room is simply a public-relations gimmick and that, somewhere, there has to be a flossy Shangri-La—or that because he's thirty-three and still not married, he doesn't like girls (he does). But as one senator from the Midwest noted . . . : "No one can really get anything on him—and it's not because they haven't tried." And no one is more aware than Nader that one crack in his credibility—or his character—and he has had it. As he once said when a lobbyist complained that Nader could make "rash" charges because he has no one to answer to: "The exact opposite is the case. I'm the one who can't afford to make mistakes."

To guard against mistakes, Nader has a hypersensitive fear of falling into compromising situations. Recently, a sultry-voiced woman from an Asian embassy somehow got hold of his unlisted number and called to inquire whether the handsome Nader would like to "come to a party and meet some girls." Nader's only response: "How did you get my number?" On another occasion, he received a letter from a man representing himself as a Ph.D. employed by a big Midwestern meat packer. The man offered Nader some extremely damaging evidence against his employer, who had been fighting the meat-inspection bill. Nader checked—and found that the Ph.D. was a phony and that any "evidence" he offered would have critically damaged Nader's credibility.

To protect that credibility, Nader doggedly researches his subject, constantly cross-checking to make sure he is not caught with his facts down. To document his case for meat inspection, for instance, he once spent sixteen straight hours copying by hand evidence from Agriculture Department archives. His room is a jumble of newspapers, yellowed congressional records and legal journals, all of which he has read or clipped but none of which he has ever bothered to throw away. That pile is increased daily by the five newspapers, ten weekly magazines and twenty monthly publications he subscribes to in his search for evidence or ideas. And to bore into problems outside of Washington, the telephone has practically become an extension of his right hand; once at a single sitting in a Chicago pay phone booth he ran up a long-distance bill totaling $85.

But Ralph Nader is not often sitting. While he must spend some hours every day in his drab, $97-a-month downtown office (the location of which he keeps secret) answering mail, writing and using the telephone, he most often is on the prowl. His skinny frame bent forward and his intense dark eyes giving him the look of a ferret, he lopes from congressional office to regulatory agency to a meeting with a reporter with information to swap. He rarely relaxes—and then in rare ways. "Oh, I like to sit down and talk about anthropology with an expert for a couple of hours," he once replied when a reporter wondered what he did for kicks.

To finance his crusade, Nader currently has only his own resources—and by the standards of most of Washington's lobbyists, they would support perhaps one medium-size cocktail party at the Shoreham. His 1965 book brought him about $50,000, but those royalties are now petering out. While he receives an average of ten invitations each week to make speeches, he accepts only about two dates a month—at $500 apiece. Last fall, he earned another $2,500 teaching a course on "corporate reform" at Princeton, his undergraduate alma mater. But that check hasn't yet arrived, and he said only half-jokingly . . . : "If it doesn't come soon, I'm going to be overdrawn." His monthly telephone bill is normally in the $200-$300 range and he spends an equal amount on books, newspapers, periodicals and other research material. He couldn't care less for material things; his wardrobe numbers four suits, he eats in cut-rate cafeterias and he owns no car.

An ascetic? Obviously. But Ralph Nader's principal quality— the one that sets him apart from most of his fellow citizens—is a well-honed sense of society's shortcomings and a practical view of what he can do about them. This is how he summed up his own view of his special mission in a recent interview with *Newsweek* correspondents in Washington:

> I'm not really a reformer; so many reformers leave a lot to be desired. A dreamer? No, I've got to be practical. But the real question is [not] why I'm doing what I'm doing but why so many people don't care. What we do about corporate air and water pollution, corporate soil and food contamination, corporate-bred trauma on the highways, corporate inflationary pricing, corporate misallocation of resources and corporate dominance over state, local and Federal agencies—to suggest a few issues—will decide the quality of our lives.

Then, in the very next breath, Nader denied he is either antibusiness or convinced that businessmen themselves are evil.

> It's a disservice to view this as a threat to the private-enterprise economy or to big business [he insisted]. It's just the opposite. It is an attempt to preserve the free-enterprise economy by making the market work better; an attempt to preserve the democratic control of technology by giving government a role in the decision-making process as to how much or how little "safety" products must contain.

Nader is nothing if not dogged in pursuit of his goals. Some think he is too abrasive as well, and too intolerant. But informally, it is hard not to like Nader. He is an engaging young man, neither boastful nor falsely modest about his fame, simply accepting it as a useful fact of his life. He is a persuasive defender of his ideals but not a bore about them. He can even kid about his own dedication; when someone urges him to turn the heat on one new industry or another, he may feign surprise and ask: "What's the matter? Do you see a conspiracy in everything?" . . .

Lloyd Cutler, an attorney and wealthy Washington lobbyist, who earned a fat fee for representing the auto industry at the ill-fated safety hearings, offers this appraisal of Nader: "He is an important and effective social and political force, but he'd be more effective if he were more charitable of the motives and integrity of the people he attacks." An industrial executive adds: "Nader's influence has been distorted out of proportion. He's a dedicated man, but his programs have become sort of a witch hunt; he's gotten a little carried away. What really is his objective? Is he going to save the American public singlehanded? People get enthralled with the idea of the fame and power that controversy can bring."

More fundamentally, there are those in Congress and business who worry that Nader may be driven to mounting attacks just to maintain his franchise as the nation's No. 1 consumer crusader. And they worry about too much power moving into the hands of someone responsible only to himself.

Nader recognizes most of these problems, and insists that they are groundless. But he has some worries of his own. Nader confesses at times to growing weary of the pace he maintains, laments that he can handle "only about four" major consumer issues at a time. He wishes he had a larger income to bankroll his efforts but is unwilling to make any compromise with his principles to raise money. Above all, he frets that Ralph Nader may eventually wear out his welcome and thus lose his unique usefulness. . . .

Some in Washington never stop wondering why Nader, now a household word, doesn't just cash in his chips and get out. "Why," one lobbyist marveled, "with his name, most people would become wealthy TV lecturers." . . .

But to Nader, the only cause worth serving remains his conception of the public interest, and he is determined to continue the fight. Last week, he was gathering evidence and charting strategy on a long list of new issues: drug safety, the sonic boom, mine safety—even the venerable and seemingly impregnable oil-depletion allowance. But for a change, the lone wolf was looking for help. By midyear, hopefully with financial help from a foundation, Nader plans to organize a "public interest" law firm in Washington, staffed with at least seven lawyers, an economist, an engineer, accountant and doctor to start making meaningful progress on what he describes as his ultimate objective: "nothing less than the qualitative reform of the industrial revolution."

THE ROLE OF COOPERATIVES [4]

The Shoppers Protest, as far as cooperatives are concerned, is entering its 124th year. Since the time of the Rochdale pioneers people have banded together economically through cooperatives to provide consumers with the opportunity to purchase quality products at the best possible price.

"Shoppers Protest Enters 123rd Year" was the headline appearing in the Bay Area, California, newspapers recently during the housewives' revolt. This ad went on to explain what has become more evident in Berkeley; Washington, D.C.; Aurora, Minnesota; and in Chicago—that cooperatives give consumers one of the best tools for a voice in the marketplace.

Cooperatives do about 3 per cent of total business in United States and most of this is in agriculture, purchasing and marketing. Significant strides have been made in agricultural cooperative growth with savings being made on the purchasing of fuels, supplies and credit. Agricultural marketing cooperatives have assisted in orderly marketing and helped farmers achieve a higher percentage of the consumer's food dollar.

Credit unions compose the largest nonfarm segment of U.S. cooperative enterprise with 14.6 million members doing nearly a billion-dollar loan volume a year. They also provide about 10 per cent of all consumer credit.

There are about 5.6 million members in other types of consumer cooperative endeavors doing about $500 million worth of business.

A true measure of potential consumer cooperative effectiveness can only be realized by venturing to Europe where in Sweden, for example, 20-25 per cent of consumer goods are purchased through cooperatives.

The important fact about a cooperative is that the customers own it and when customers own and support their cooperative, they can be sure that it meets their needs. Membership in a co-

[4] "Cooperatives; How Can Cooperatives Help the Consumer Solve His Problem?" excerpts from address at 1967 New York Consumer Assembly by Stanley Dreyer, president of the Cooperative League of the U.S.A. *Co-Op Contact* (publication of the United Housing Foundation). 8 no 2:CC12. Spring '67. Reprinted by permission.

operative is open to all; each member has one vote in the affairs of his cooperative. He usually contributes to capital in proportion to his patronage and shares in earnings based on patronage.

Cooperatives are user-oriented. Most business today is production-oriented. The consumers' revolt, the age of the more enlightened consumer, I feel, portends greater opportunity, greater possibilities and greater success for consumer cooperatives.

All of us are consumers. We are consumers of many different things. In our society we have put more collective effort into increasing income than we have been concerned about constructively using those hard-earned dollars. Heretofore, the consumer could cast his individual vote in the marketplace. But I contend that any family with a television set no longer enters the supermarket maze without pre-established subconscious psychological influences at work of "doves in the kitchen," "giants in the closet" or "knights in shining armor."

The time is ripe for consumers to join forces—to become more adequately informed and responsibly mobilize their efforts in economic self-help cooperatives.

Cooperatives do a number of things which help the consumer solve his problems.

1. Cooperatives help people identify their needs, whether it be for good homes in good neighborhoods at prices people can afford; or whether it be for quality products at reasonable prices.

2. Cooperatives help people organize their needs, such as the Puerto Rican housewives on the lower east side [of New York City] who organized their buying power in Portorriquenos Unidos with savings up to 9 per cent per year on their food purchases. Cooperatives help people organize a need for its fulfillment and not for profit.

3. Cooperatives give consumers not only the voice in the marketplace but give the consumer economic power. When consumers join together in a united effort they can do something about supermarket gimmicks, and can lower the cost of funerals, for example, up to 75 per cent.

Cooperative supermarkets not only have joined the buying power of individual neighbors, but they have joined into area federations to take advantage of management skills, economies of size and increased buying power. Mid-Eastern Cooperatives has just completed a fine new grocery warehouse to buy merchandise at more reasonable costs and effect lower total distribution costs. Mid-Eastern, along with other regional cooperative warehouses, joins its buying power with similar groups through a national cooperative quality-conscious buyer organization.

4. Cooperatives assure quality, instill confidence and bring honesty to the marketplace. They have no other objective than to operate on a sound business basis in order to provide their users with quality products and dependable services at the best value.

5. Cooperatives strive to serve the consumer at cost. Forward-looking cooperatives, properly managed and adequately financed, are one of the most efficient ways for consumers to get the goods and services they want.

6. Cooperatives strive to inform the consumer to be a better buyer. Since cooperatives are owned by the people they serve, the financial gain and operating records are publicly disclosed at regular membership meetings. Cooperative publications traditionally perform a continuous education function on behalf of consumers. Operating in the consumer's interest they have nothing to hide.

7. Cooperatives strive to promote the consumers' interest through their various trade associations which encourage positive legislation and administrative rulings in the fields of interest to consumers.

BIBLIOGRAPHY

An asterisk (*) preceding a reference indicates that the article or a part of it has been reprinted in this book.

BOOKS, PAMPHLETS, AND DOCUMENTS

AFL-CIO Department of Legislation. Labor looks at Congress 1967, an AFL-CIO legislative report. (Publication no 77-I) American Federation of Labor and Congress of Industrial Organizations. 815 16th St. N.W. Washington, D.C. 20006. '68.
Consumer problems. p 38-43.

Alexander, G. J. Honesty and competition. Syracuse University Press. Syracuse, N.Y. '67.

Backman, Jules. Advertising and competition. New York University Press. New York. '67.

Bauer, R. A. and Greyser, S. A. Advertising in America: the consumer view. Harvard University. Graduate School of Business Administration. Boston. '67.

Chapman, J. M. and Shay, R. P. eds. Consumer finance industry: its costs and regulation. Columbia University Press. New York. '67.

*Consumer Advisory Council. Consumer issues '66; report to the President. General Services Administration. Washington, D.C. 20405. '66.

Consumer Reports Editors. Consumers Union report on life insurance. Harper. New York. '68.

Fargis, Paul. Consumer's handbook. Hawthorn. New York. '67.

*Freedom of Information Conference, 9th, University of Missouri, 1966. Freedom of information in the market place. Ovid Bell Press. Fulton, Mo. '67.
Reprinted in this book: Business ethics and consumer protection. V. H. Nyborg. p 49-56.

Furness, Betty. Consumer's interest in advertising; address to the Association of National Advertisers workshop, Hot Springs, West Virginia, October 29-November 1, 1967. The Association. 155 E. 44th St. New York 10017. '67.

*Furness, Betty. Remarks of the Special Assistant to the President for Consumer Affairs, before the National Retail Merchants Association, New York City, January 9, 1968. Mimeo. The Author. The White House Office. Washington, D.C. 20500. '68.

Gilboy, E. W. Primer on the economics of consumption. Random House. New York. '68.

Keeton, R. E. and O'Connell, Jeffrey. After cars crash; the need for legal and insurance reforms. Dow Jones-Irwin. Homewood, Ill. '67.

*Lefkowitz, L. J. Consumer protection by state legislation; address before New York State Bar Association, Antitrust Law Section, January 26, 1967, New York City. The Author. 80 Centre St. New York 10013. '67.

McClellan, G. S. ed. Safety on the road. (Reference Shelf. v 38, no 1) Wilson. New York. '66.

McQuade, L. C. Bridge building; an address to the Association of National Advertisers workshop, Hot Springs, West Virginia, October 29-November 1, 1967. The Association. 155 E. 44th St. New York 10017. '67.

Magnuson, W. G. and Carper, Jean. Dark side of the marketplace: the plight of the American consumer. Prentice-Hall. Englewood, N.J. '68.

Margolius, Sidney. Buyer, be wary. (Pamphlet no 382) Public Affairs Committee. 381 Park Ave. S. New York 10016. '65.

Margolius, Sidney. Consumer's guide to health insurance plans. (Pamphlet no 325) Public Affairs Committee. 381 Park Ave. S. New York 10016. '62.

Margolius, Sidney. Family money problems. (Pamphlet no 412) Public Affairs Committee. 381 Park Ave. S. New York 10016. '67.

Margolius, Sidney. Funeral costs and death benefits. (Pamphlet no 409) Public Affairs Committee. 381 Park Ave. S. New York 10016. '67.

Margolius, Sidney. Guide to consumer credit. (Pamphlet no 348) Public Affairs Committee. 381 Park Ave. S. New York 10016. '63.

Margolius, Sidney. Innocent consumer vs. the exploiters. Simon & Schuster. New York. '67.

*Marshall, M. L. FTC and deceptive advertising. (Freedom of Information Center Report no 183) University of Missouri. School of Journalism. Columbia. '67.

Metcalf, Lee and Reinemer, Vic. Overcharge. McKay. New York. '67.

Mintz, Morton. By prescription only; a report on the roles of the U.S. Food and Drug Administration, the American Medical Association, pharmaceutical manufacturers and others in connection with the irrational and massive use of prescription drugs that may be worthless, injurious, or even lethal. 2d ed. Beacon Press. Boston. '67.

Mowbray, A. Q. The thumb on the scale; or, the supermarket shell game. Lippincott. New York. '67.

Nader, Ralph. Unsafe at any speed; the designed-in dangers of the American automobile. Grossman. New York. '65.

*Nelson, Gaylord. Remarks to Consumer's Assembly, Washington, D.C., November 2, 1967. The Author. Senate Office Bldg. Washington, D.C. 20510. '67.

New York Consumer Assembly. Digest of proceedings, New York Consumer Assembly, January 14, 1967. The Assembly. 465 Grand St. New York 10002. '67.

*O'Connell, Jeffrey. Crises in car insurance—cause and cure; remarks at AMA briefing Modernizing Insurance Marketing Plans, August 24, 1967, New York City. mimeo. American Management Association. Press Relations Department. 135 W. 50th St. New York 10020. '67.

Stewart, G. R. Not so rich as you think. Houghton. Boston. '68.

Stewart, W. H. Consumer rights and responsibilities; an address to the Consumer Assembly 1967, Washington, D.C., November 2, 1967. United States. Department of Health, Education, and Welfare. Washington, D.C. 20201. '67.

Tincher, W. R. Government and business . . . perspective for tomorrow; an address to the Association of National Advertisers workshop, San Diego, California, March 2-4, 1967. The Association. 155 E. 44th St. New York 10017. '67.

*Turner, D. F. Advertising and competition; an address before the Briefing Conference on Federal Controls of Advertising and Promotion sponsored by the Federal Bar Association and the Foundation of the Federal Bar Association in cooperation with the Bureau of National Affairs, Inc., June 2, 1966, Washington, D.C. mimeo. The Author. United States Department of Justice. Washington, D.C. 20530. '66.

United States. Congress. House of Representatives. Committee on the Judiciary. Automobile insurance study; a report by the staff of the Antitrust subcommittee (Subcommittee no 5). (House Report no 815) 90th Congress, 1st session. Supt. of Docs. Washington, D.C. 20402. '67.

United States. Congress. Senate. Committee on Banking and Currency. Truth in lending, 1967; report to accompany S. 5, together with individual views; June 29, 1967. Senate Document Room. The Capitol. Washington, D.C. 20510. '67.

United States. Department of Agriculture. Consumers all; the yearbook of agriculture. Supt. of Docs. Washington, D.C. 20402. '65.

United States. Department of Health, Education, and Welfare. Report to the President on medical care prices. Supt. of Docs. Washington, D.C. 20402. '67.

Wilhelms, F. T. and Heimerl, R. P. Consumer economics. 3d ed. McGraw. New York. '66.

PERIODICALS

American Federationist. 73:12-16. My. '66. Jigsaw puzzle of health care.
H. K. Abrams.

*American Federationist. 74:1-4. Ap. '67. Consumer rights: the battle
continues. Sidney Margolius.

American Federationist. 74:5-9. D. '67. Auto insurance: the need for
reform. Sidney Margolius.

BioScience. 17:864. D. '67. Consumer reports for scientists. Lester
Goldstein.

*Business Week. p 84-6. D. 23, '67. Consumers Union puts on muscle.

Commonweal. 86:332-3. Je. 9, '67. Back to the dance; Senate hearings
on high price of drugs.

*Congressional Digest. 47:65-96. Mr. '68. Congress & consumer protec-
tion proposals: pro and con.
          Reprinted in this book: The scope of present Federal activity. p 68-70.

Consumer Bulletin. 48:39-40. N. '65. U.S.D.A.'s role as the consumer's
adviser.

Consumer Bulletin. 50:31-2. Ja. '67. Year of the consumer.

*Consumer Bulletin. 50:4+. O. '67. X-ray hazard in TV sets.

*Consumer Bulletin. 50:19-20. N. '67. Post Office protects consumers
against fraud.

Consumer Reports. 31:571-3. N. '66. 30th, a year to remember.

*Consumer Reports. 32:113-15. F. '67. Some truth-in-packaging . . .
but not enough.
          Excerpts: Co-Op News. 2:3-4. Winter '67.

*Consumer Reports. 32:470-4. S. '67. Big hole in truth-in-lending.

Consumer Reports. 33:9-15. Ja. '68. Auto insurance reform; basic
protection plan.

Co-Op Contact. 8 no 2:CC5-6. Spring '67. Medical care. M. L. Gross.

*Co-Op Contact. 8 no 2:CC7+. Spring '67. Consumer problems of
the poor. David Caplovitz.

*Co-Op Contact. 8 no 2:CC-12. Spring '67. Cooperatives: how can
cooperatives help the consumer solve his problem? excerpts [from
address at 1967 New York Consumer Assembly]. Stanley Dreyer.

Co-Op Contact. 9 no 1:CC3-4+. Winter '67. Primacy of the consumer.
H. M. Kallen.

*Co-Op Contact. 9 no 1:CC4-5+. Winter '67. Ralph Nader faces the
nation's business. Ralph Nader.

Fortune. 73:128-31+. Mr. '66. Antitrust in an era of radical change.
Max Ways.

Fortune. 75:110-15+. Mr. '67. U.S. economy enters a new era. William
Bowen.

*Fortune. 76:118-20+. S. 1, '67. Welcome to the consumption com-
munity. D. J. Boorstin.

*Fortune. 76:114-17+. D. '67. Diverse $10,000-and-over masses. L. A. Mayer.

Harvard Business Review. 45:79-86. Ja. '67. Marketing ethics & the consumer. E. A. Clasen.

*Harvard Business Review. 45:2-4+. N. '67. Dialogue that never happens. R. A. Bauer and S. A. Greyser.

Journal of Public Law. 16 no 2:296-325. '67. How much truth in what kinds of lending? J. A. Spanogle, Jr.

Michigan Law Review. 64:1197-348. My. '66. Symposium on consumer protection.

Michigan Law Review. 66:81-114. N. '67. Regulation of finance charges on consumer instalment credit. R. W. Johnson.

New Leader. 50:15-17. O. 9, '67. Breaking the "Birch Rod." J. A. Ruskay.

New Republic. 153:7. Ag. 21, '65. Fleecing the consumer; fraud cases in the slums.

New Republic. 157:15-16. Ag. 19, '67. Watch that hamburger. Ralph Nader.

New Republic. 158:19-21. Ja. 6, '68. Something fishy. Ralph Nader.

New York Post. p 27. F. 17, '68. Truth in lending. Ray Wilkins.

*New York Times. p 57. My. 22, '67. F.D.A. toughens regulations for ads on prescription drugs.

New York Times. p 69+. O. 23, '67. Personal finance: varied group joins Family Service to advise consumer bogged in debt. E. M. Fowler.

*New York Times. p 1+. O. 25, '67. A family's needs found 50% higher. D. R. Jones.

New York Times. p 25+. O. 29, '67. Ralph Nader crusade; or, the rise of a self-appointed lobbyist.

*New York Times. p 1F+. N. 12, '67. Legislators study bills on abuses. Isadore Barmash.

*New York Times. p 14F. N. 12, '67. Customers encounter non-response. Lee Kanner.

New York Times. p 29. N. 16, '67. Administration stiffens stand on meat inspection. W. M. Blair.

New York Times. p 1+. N. 21, '67. Johnson appeals for consumer aid. Roy Reed.

New York Times. p 25. N. 23, '67. House panel bars credit cost plan. Marjorie Hunter.

New York Times. p 1+. N. 25, '67. Legislators, shopping in Harlem, confirm consumers' complaints. Deirdre Carmody.

New York Times. p 1+. N. 25, '67. Trust action charges restraint on advertising funeral prices. W. M. Blair.

*New York Times. p 37. D. 4, '67. Miss Furness sets education drive. J. D. Morris.

New York Times. p 1+. D. 6, '67. Conferees adopt Senate meat bill to lift standard. W. M. Blair.

New York Times. p 1+. D. 18, '67. Auto insurance facing inquiries. Wallace Turner.

New York Times. p 35. D. 19, '67. Auto insurance barred to many as companies seek to cut losses. Wallace Turner.

New York Times. p 35. D. 19, '67. Auto policies vary little among the companies.

New York Times. p 1+. D. 31, '67. Goddard expects ban on 300 drugs. R. D. Lyons.

New York Times. p 16. Ja. 18, '68. Transcript of President's message to Congress.
        Section on consumer legislation.

New York Times. p 19. Ja. 18, '68. President seeks aid to consumers. J. D. Morris.

New York Times. p 1+. Ja. 22, '68. Auto safety recall drive: Detroit critics heartened. J. M. Flint.

New York Times. p 1+. Ja. 24, '68. 3,600 drugs facing relabeling to list ailments they combat.

New York Times. p 39. Ja. 25, '68. House panel clears bill to let buyers know credit cost.

*New York Times. p 1+. F. 7, '68. President offers 8-point program to aid consumers. J. D. Morris.

New York Times. p 50. F. 18, '68. Insurance shift sought in Boston. J. H. Fenton.

*New York Times. p 25. F. 23, 68. Betty Furness wins over critics in her job. Nan Robertson.

New York Times. p 1+. My. 23, '68. Congress passes "truth in lending."

New York Times Magazine. p 26-7+. Ag. 27, '67. Next: a new auto insurance policy. D. P. Moynihan.

*Newsweek. 71:65-7+. Ja. 22, '68. Meet Ralph Nader.

Science. 152:332-3. Ap. 15, '66. FDA's edict: patients, not profits, come first; excerpts from address, April 6, 1966. J. L. Goddard.

*Time. 91:20-1. Ja. 26, '68. Business with 103 million unsatisfied customers.

Trial. 3:10-53. O. '67. Special issue: Auto insurance; the great debate.

Vital Speeches of the Day. 33:179-84. Ja. 1, '67. National traffic safety agency; address, November 29, 1966. William Haddon, Jr.

*Vital Speeches of the Day. 33:189-92. Ja. 1, '67. The consumer; address, December 6, 1966. L. E. Skinner.

*Vital Speeches of the Day. 33:247-52. F. 1, '67. Who best speaks for the consumer? address, September 20, 1966. M. E. Brunk.

Vital Speeches of the Day. 33:364-8. Ap. 1, '67. Standards and the public interest; address, February 13, 1967. J. H. Hollomon.

Vital Speeches of the Day. 34:230-1. F. 1, '68. Food prices; address, January 13, 1968. G. L. Mehren.

Wall Street Journal. p 1+. S. 5, '67. Insurers under fire. Stanford Sesser.

*Wall Street Journal. p 26. N. 24, '67. Soft-treatment for Jell-O: self-regulation of food products' purity by processors is aim of new FDA project. Jonathan Spivak.

Wall Street Journal. p 30. Ja. 11, '68. Hue due at HEW: Gardner plans to reshape agency to stress consumer needs; outcry by lobbies likely. Jonathan Spivak.

*Wall Street Journal. p 1+. Ja. 12, '68. With a prod by Nader, U.S. mulls a clean-up of fish processors. F. L. Zimmerman.